Śrī Śrī Guru Gaurāṅgau Jayataḥ

Ekādaśī Māhātmya

The Glories of Ekādaśī

Translated by

Bhumipati Dāsa

Edited by

Puṇḍarīka Vidyānidhi Dāsa

Other Publications

Gauracandra (Part 1 & 2)—Coloring book
Govinda (Part 1)—Coloring book
Gokula—Coloring book
Ayodhya—Coloring book
Sri Harinama Cintamani
Sri Manah-siksa
Sri Siksastaka
The Bhakti Trilogy
Prema Vivarta

ISBN 81-87812-00-1

RASBIHARI LAL & SONS

Published by:

Rasbihari Lal & Sons
Loi Bazar, Vrindavan-281121
Phone: 0565-442570
Fax: 0565-443092
Our other division Brijwasi Exports

Printed at:

Ekādaśī Māhātmya

Introduction

By the unlimited mercy of the most merciful Lord Śrī Kṛṣṇa this book *Ekādaśī Māhātmya* has been published. By studying the glorious subject matter of this book the faith of persons observing the vows of Ekādaśī will be strengthened. Moreover, persons who are inquisitive about this subject matter will obtain the light of knowledge from this book.

This particular book, however, does not discuss the complete truth regarding Śrī Ekādaśī. The glories of observing Ekādaśī are being described in this book through the presentation of stories. Some people may interpret or imagine that the glories described in this book are simply an exaggeration, or they may think that observing Ekādaśī is simply meant for achieving material happiness and prosperity. Śrī Ekādaśī, which falls on the eleventh day of each waxing and waning moon, is very dear to Lord Hari. That is why this day is also known as Hari-vāsara. A proper and elaborate explanation about Ekādaśī is given in *Śrī Hari-bhakti-vilāsa*. In fact one should observe Ekādaśī only to please the Supreme Lord. It is stated in the scriptures:

ekādaśī vratam nāma sarva kāma phala pradam
kartavyam sarvadā viprair viṣṇu prīṇana kāraṇam

"The *brāhmaṇas* should always observe Ekādaśī to please Lord Viṣṇu for this fulfills all one's desires. Therefore everyone should observe the vow of Ekādaśī for the sake of satisfying the Lord. Then happiness and prosperity will automatically follow." It is stated in *Bṛhan-nāradīya Purāṇa* that if everyone including the *brāhmaṇas*, the *kṣatriyas*, the *vaiśyas*, the *śūdras* and the women observe Ekādaśī they will certainly attain liberation. Although various temporary results are found in the scriptures for following the vow of Ekādaśī, which is one of the limbs of regulative devotional service, nevertheless one should know that the principle fruit of devotional service is to develop intense love for the Supreme Lord. Even if the four objectives of life namely religiosity, economic development, sense gratification, and liberation automatically follow the performer, still the unalloyed pure devotees don't fall prey to this; rather they abandon these objectives and achieve love of God which is the fifth objective of life.

Since the living entities of Kali-yuga are short-lived and lusty, they are unable to perform severe austerity. The living entities of Kali-yuga subsist mainly on food grains and they cannot survive without eating grains, whereas the people of Satya, Tretā, and Dvāpara-yugas were capable of undergoing severe austerities and tolerating physical distresses. Thus a minimum austerity in the form of fasting twice a month on the days of Ekādaśī has been prescribed for the people of Kali-yuga. If possible, they should eat only once the day before Ekādaśī, fast totally on the day of Ekādaśī, and eat only once the day after Ekādaśī. If one is unable to follow even this, in other words if one is unable to eat only once on the day before and after Ekādaśī, then he must observe complete fast on the day of Ekādaśī. If one is still unable to follow this, then he should give up eating five types of grains and observe the vow of Ekādaśī simply by partaking of some fruits and roots. It is stated in *Mahābhārata Udyoga-parva* quoted in *Hari-bhakti-vilāsa* 12.40 as follows.

aṣṭaitānyavrataghnani āpo mūlam phalam payaḥ
havir brāhmaṇa kāmyā ca guror vacanam auṣadham'e,

"Water, fruits, roots, milk, ghee, satisfying a *brāhmaṇa*, following the instruction of the spiritual master, and medicine—these eight items don't break one's vow of Ekādaśī."

Since grave sinful reactions equal to that of killing a *brāhmaṇa* or a cow take shelter within five types of grains on the day of Ekādaśī, persons who desire ultimate benefit give up eating these grains on this day. The five types of grains are 1. rice or other products made from rice such as flat rice, puffed rice etc., 2. wheat flour and white flour etc., 3. barley etc., 4. pulses such as moong, chickpea, green peas, lentil, etc. 5. mustard oil and sesame oil. If one eats any of the above-mentioned grains then his vow of Ekādaśī will be broken.

Another name of Ekādaśī is Hari-vāsara because the main purpose of observing Ekādaśī is to totally please Lord Hari with all one's senses. In other words one should try to please Lord Hari and the devotees of Hari. The meaning of the word *upavāsa* (fasting) is to live nearby. On the day of Ekādaśī one should remain aloof from all kinds of sinful activities, give up all kinds of household activities and sense gratification and live near the Lord. It is stated in *Hari-bhakti-vilāsa* 13.14, which is quoted from *Gṛhya-pariśiṣṭa*, *Kātyāna-smṛti*, *Viṣṇu-dharma*, and *Brahma-vaivarta Purāṇa*:

upāvṛttasya pāpebhyo yas tu vāso guṇaiḥ saha
upavāsaḥ sa vijñeyaḥ sarva bhoga vivarjitaḥ

"The word *upavāsa*, or fasting, refers to staying aloof from all kinds of sinful activities and sense gratification."

Lord Hari is the transcendental Personality of Godhead and is beyond the three modes of material nature. It is not possible to live with Him by the help of one's material body, mind, and intelligence. Every conditioned soul is covered by two bodies, namely gross and subtle. Therefore how can they live with the Lord? Observing the vow of Ekādaśī is one of the principle limbs among the sixty-four limbs of devotional service described by Śrīla Rupa Gosvāmīpāda, an associate of Śrīman Mahāprabhu. Among the sixty-four limbs of devotional service the first and foremost is to take shelter of a bona fide spiritual master. Without taking shelter of the lotus feet of the bona fide spiritual master, who is well conversant with the scripture, attached to the Absolute Truth and very dear to Śrī Hari, one cannot engage in worshiping Śrī Hari. When one surrenders to the lotus feet of the spiritual master, then by his mercy and empowerment one's material pride is destroyed and his pure spiritual constitutional position is revived. As a result he becomes qualified to serve the Supreme Lord through his service-inclined senses, or in other words, he becomes qualified to live with the Lord. The mind is the cause of a living entity's bondage or liberation. If one cannot convert the function of the mind into a favorable condition for devotional service, then one cannot live with the Lord. Thus it is extremely necessary to associate with pure devotees in order to convert the averse mind into a service-inclined mind. Without being subordinate to the devotees of the Lord one cannot live with the Lord, even if he engages in various external ritualistic activities. For this reason there is gulf of difference between the karmic observation of Ekādaśī and the devotees' observation. It is stated in *Caitanya-caritāmṛta* (*Madhya* 22.51) as follows:

mahat-kṛpā vinā kona karme 'bhakti' naya
kṛṣṇa-bhakti dūre rahu, saṁsāra nahe kṣaya

"Unless one is favored by a pure devotee, he cannot attain the platform of devotional service. To say nothing of *kṛṣṇa-bhakti*, one cannot even be relieved from the bondage of material existence."

Those who observe the vow of Ekādaśī are divided into three categories.

1. The majority of the people of this world consider their gross and subtle bodies as their self. They think that the rules and regulations of the scriptures and the prescription of the sages are meant for protecting the self-interest of their gross bodies. They are doubtful about the existence of the soul and thus give more importance to self interest of the body. Their conception is that if the soul exists at all it is simply for the sake of the gross body.

2. Although these people believe that the constitutional position of a living entity is that he is a spirit soul, not the body, and that the Supreme Lord is the cause of the living entities and it is the duty of a living entity to worship the Supreme Lord, nevertheless they consider both the deliverance of the soul and happiness of the body to be the goal of life. Therefore they think that the scriptural prescriptions such as observing Ekādaśī are meant for both deliverance of the soul and protection of the body's self interest.

3. However, some people in the minority say that a living entity is constitutionally part and parcel of the Supreme Lord, eternal, full of knowledge, and blissful. The two coverings in the form of gross and subtle bodies are attributed to the living entities by the external energy of the Lord, hence unwanted. Since the gross and subtle bodies are born from the external energy of the Lord, the Supreme

Lord is naturally the enjoyer and proprietor of those bodies. In other words, the soul, the mind and the body of a living entity all belong to Kṛṣṇa. Therefore it is the only duty of the soul, mind and body to fully engage in the service of the Lord. By worshiping Lord Hari one's own and others' benefit is accomplished. Execution of pure devotional service is the only means of attaining eternal peace. In order to please the Supreme Lord only they cultivate the limbs of pure devotional service such as observing the vow of Ekādaśī. They know that the principle purpose of all these practices is to achieve love of God. They also know that these limbs of devotional service are not prescribed for material sense gratification or protecting the self interest of the gross and subtle bodies. The pure devotees who follow in the foot steps of Śrī Caitanya respect this consideration which is based on pure devotional service.

Some people, particularly many devotees from Jagannātha Purī in Orissa, say that there is no fault in accepting grain *mahā-prasāda* of Jagannātha on Ekādaśī. But the point of consideration at this juncture is that the Vaiṣṇavas don't accept anything other than *mahā-prasāda* regularly. Therefore in order to protect the prestige of Ekādaśī they offer obeisances to the *mahā-prasāda* and save it for the next day. Śrīla Bhaktisiddhanta Sarasvatī Gosvāmī Prabhupāda has given the following explanation in his *Anubhaṣya* commentary on the fifteenth chapter of *Ādi-līlā* of *Śrī Caitanya-caritāmṛta*: "Śrī Mahāprabhu said that if one disregards the vow of Ekādaśī he brings ruination to his life. One should simply respect the grain *prasāda* on the day of Ekādaśī and save it for the next day, for the effect of Ekādaśī no longer remains on the next day. The pious Vaiṣṇavas are simply satisfied by drinking the nectar of Kṛṣṇa's holy names on the day of Ekādaśī. They do not indulge in any kind of sense gratification, do not speak useless topics and they abandon all kinds of material enjoyment. Honoring *prasāda* is an eternal activity of the pure Vaiṣṇavas and they never eat anything that is not first offered to the Lord. The devotees should totally fast on the day of Ekādaśī and eat the Lord's remnants only on the next day. In a special case a Vaiṣṇava may take non-grain remnants of the Lord. Those who are non-Vaiṣṇavas engage in sense gratification day and night on the pretext of honoring *prasāda*.

Such people associate with sinful men, eat grain on Ekādaśī and disrespect the vow of Ekādaśī. If you cultivate the limbs of devotional service with respect, then you will attain the mercy of Bhakti Devi. Give up the association of nondevotees and strictly observe the vow of Ekādaśī by engaging in chanting the holy names of the Supreme Lord."

It has been repeatedly declared in the *Purāṇas* that one should not eat on the day of Ekādaśī. It is stated in *Viṣṇu-smṛti* that all the sinful reactions such as killing a *brāhmaṇa* take shelter in the food grain, therefore if one eats grain on the day of Ekādaśī he certainly eats sin. There is no arrangement of atonement for the deliverance of a person who eats grain on Ekādaśī, in other words according to the gravity of a sinful activity various arrangements for atonement are prescribed by the twenty dharma *śāstras*, but eating grain on Ekādaśī is so grave a sin that there is no atonement prescribed for this.

Persons who desire to cultivate pure devotional service should carefully remember the following consideration while following the vow of Ekādaśī. The Vaiṣṇavas don't observe any vow or festival on a particular day which is perforated with the previous *tithi* or day. In such a case they observe the vow or festival on the next day. According to Vedic calculation a day starts with the sun rise. If the day of Daśamī continues up to the one and half hours before the sunrise of the next day even then the Ekādaśī should not be observed on the next day rather it should be observed the day after. In this regard we quote some authentic scriptural statements found in *Śrī Hari-bhakti-vilāsa*, the king of Vaiṣṇava *smṛtis,* as follows:

"O *brāhmaṇa*, if the day of Ekādaśī starts ninety-six minutes before the sunrise then it is pure Ekādaśī. A householder should fast on such an Ekādaśī." [*Garuḍa Purāṇa*]

"If the *tithi,* or day of Ekādaśī, begins one hour thirty-six minutes before the sunrise then it is called a complete Ekādaśī and if the Ekādaśī starts less then one hour thirty-six minutes before the sunrise then it should be considered incomplete and contaminated because it is perforated with the previous *tithi.* Therefore one should give up the following of Ekādaśī if it is mixed with the previous *tithi* at the time of sunrise. Particularly the

Vaiṣṇavas should totally abandon following the vow of such an Ekādaśī. The great sage Kanva said, 'If the day of Ekādaśī is mixed with the previous *tithi* then one should fast on the next day for Ekādaśī and break fast on the following day.'" [*Bhaviṣya Purāṇa*]

"Usually the days begin from the rising of the sun and are complete on the next rising of the sun. But this is not the case with Ekādaśī. If an Ekādaśī starts one hour thirty-six minutes before the sunrise then only is it uncontaminated and complete." [*Skanda Purāṇa*]

We request all the kind-hearted readers to study this book with special attention.

Notes on Ekādaśī

Standard for Ekādaśī break fasts.

If you have observed a complete fast (without even water) you do not need to break it with grains, you can break it with caranamrita or fruit. But if you have observed Ekādaśī by eating fruit and vegetables etc. then it should be broken the following day by taking grains at the right times.
Mahadvadasi is observed like Ekādaśī.

Ekādaśī
The essence is to eat simply, once or twice, so that one can spend as much time as possible hearing, chanting and remembering Sri Sri Radha-Krsna. Never eat onions, garlic, carrots and red dahl, meat, fish or eggs, or products thereof.

Foods that are restricted during Ekādaśī:
— Tomatoes, eggplants, cauliflower, broccoli, bellpepper
— Peas, chickpeas and all types of beans, including products made from beans [papadams, tofu, tempeh, grain beverages, etc.].
— Indian vegetable: karela (bitter lemon), loki, parmal, toroi, kunli, drumsticks, okra (lady fingers), banana flower.
— All leafy vegetables: spinach, salads, cabbages and leafy herbs like parsley, curry leaves, neem leaves, etc.
— Grains: millet, barley, farina, dalia, pasta, rice, corn, all types of dahl and all types of flour made from grains and beans (like rice flour, chickpea flour, urad dahl flour, etc.)

— Starches from corn or grains and products made from and mixed with these starches like: baking soda, baking powder, certain soft drinks, custard, certain yogurts, puddings, cream cheese, sweets, candies and tapioca-balls.
— Oils made from grains: corn oil, mustard oil, sesame oil etc. and products fried in these oils: nuts, potato chips certain snack foods.
— Honey: Do not use any cooking ingredients that might be mixed with grains, such as ghee that has been used to fry puris, or spices touched by hands dusted with capati flour.

Spices that are used on Ekādaśī are: turmeric, black pepper, ginger and salt [rock salt] taken from a new or clean package.

Foods that can be taken in Ekādaśī.
— All fruits (fresh and dried), all nuts and oils made from nuts.
— Potatoes, pumpkin, cucumber, radish, squash (but no loki), green papaya, lemon, jackfruit, avocado, olives, coconut, buckwheat, all sugars. All milk products.

Mahaprasada on Ekādaśī

On Ekādaśī, strick followers of Vaisnava regulations avoid eating any mahaprasada from an offering that includes grains. Sastra explains that the papa-purusa (sin personified) takes shelter in grains on Ekādaśī, and therefore we avoid grains at all cost on that day, not even risking taking non-grain preparations of mahaprasada from an offering plate containing grains. Ekādaśī mahaprasada should be stored until the next day; if that is not possible it can be distributed to persons not strictly following Vaisnava regulations or to animals. In fact, mahaprasada maintains its purity on Ekādaśī despite the presence of the papa-purusa, and therefore it will purify anyone who eats it. Nevertheless, the followers of Caitanya Mahaprabhu, being strict followers of Vaisnava regulations, avoid mahaprasada on that day because their strict sadhana will be hampered by the presence of the papa-purusa.

Table of contents

Chapter 1 1
Utpannā Ekādaśī—during the waning moon of November/December

Chapter 2 5
Mokṣadā Ekādaśī—during the waxing moon of November/December

Chapter 3 7
Saphalā Ekādaśī—during the waning moon of December/January

Chapter 4 9
Putradā Ekādaśī—during the waxing moon of December/January

Chapter 5 13
Ṣaṭ-tilā Ekādaśī—during the waning moon of January/February

Chapter 6 17
Jayā Ekādaśī—during the waxing moon of January/February

Chapter 7 21
Vijayā Ekādaśī—during the waning moon of February/March

Chapter 8 25
Āmalakī Ekādaśī—during the waxing moon of February/March

Chapter 9 29
Pāpamocanī Ekādaśī—during the waning moon of March/April

Chapter 10 33
Kāmada Ekādaśī—during the waxing moon of March/April

Chapter 11 37
Varuthinī Ekādaśī—during the waning moon of April/May

Chapter 12 39
Mohinī Ekādaśī—during the waxing moon of April/May

Chapter 13 43
Aparā Ekādaśī—during the waning moon of May/June

Chapter 14 45
Nirjalā Ekādaśī—during the waxing moon of May/June

Chapter 15 49
Yoginī Ekādaśī—during the waning moon of June/July

Chapter 16 53
Śayanā Ekādaśī—during the waxing moon of June/July

Chapter 17 59
Kāmikā Ekādaśī—during the waning moon of July/August

Chapter 18 61
Pavitrā Ekādaśī—during the waxing moon of July/August

Chapter 19 65
Annadā Ekādaśī—during the waning moon of August/September

Chapter 20 67
Pārśva Ekādaśī—during the waxing moon of August/September

Chapter 21 69
Indirā Ekādaśī—during the waning moon of September/October

Chapter 22 73
Pāśāṅkuśā Ekādaśī—during the waxing moon of September/October

Chapter 23 75
Ramā Ekādaśī—during the waning moon of October/November

Chapter 24 79
Utthāna Ekādaśī—during the waxing moon of October/November

Chapter 25 83
Padminī Ekādaśī—during the waxing moon of the Adhika Masa

Chapter 26 87
Parama Ekādaśī—during the waning moon of the Adhika Masa

Appendix 91

Śrī Śrī Guru Gaurāṅgau Jayataḥ

Ekādaśī Māhātmya

Once in the great assembly of the sages, the renowned scholar and sage Śrī Sūta Gosvāmī made a declaration about the twenty-six Ekādaśīs. There are two Ekādaśīs in each month, making twenty-four Ekādaśīs in a year. Apart from them there are two more Ekādaśīs that occur in the extra month that comes after every two and half years. The names of the twenty four Ekādaśīs are as follows: Utpannā, Mokṣadā, Saphalā, Putradā, Ṣaṭ-tilā, Jayā, Vijayā, Āmalakī, Pāpamocanī, Kāmadā, Varuthinī, Mohinī, Aparā, Nirjalā, Yoginī, Śayanā, Kāmikā, Pavitrā, Annadā, Pārśva, Indirā, Pāśāṅkuśā, Ramā, and Utthāna Ekādaśī. The names of the two extra Ekādaśīs are Padminī and Parama. In that assembly, the glories of all the Ekādaśīs were properly sung. Those who are unable to observe Ekādaśī can get the result of observing Ekādaśī by hearing and singing their glories.

Chapter 1

Utpannā Ekādaśī

The glories of Utpannā Ekādaśī are described in the *Bhaviṣyottara Purāṇa* in a conversation between Śrī Kṛṣṇa and Arjuna. Śrī Sūta Gosvāmī said to the assembled *brāhmaṇas* and sages: "If a person with faith and devotion duly follows or hears about the glories, rules and regulations of observing Ekādaśī as described by Lord Kṛṣṇa, then he will attain happiness in this life and will return to the abode of Lord Viṣṇu in the next life."

Once Arjuna asked Śrī Kṛṣṇa, "O Janārdana, please explain to me what the benefit is of total fasting, eating only at night, or eating once at midday on Ekādaśī ?"

In reply to this, Lord Śrī Kṛṣṇa said, "O Arjuna! In the beginning of autumn on the Ekādaśī that occurs during the waning moon in the month of November-December a person should begin observing the vow of Ekādaśī. In the early morning on the day of Ekādaśī he should make a vow to observe fasting. At mid-day he should purify himself by taking a bath. At the time of taking bath he should pray as follows: 'O Asvakrante! O Rathakrante! O Viṣṇukrante! O Vasundhare! O Mrittike! O Mother earth! Please destroy all my sinful reactions accumulated from previous lifetimes so that I can attain the supreme destination.' After completing his bath he should worship Lord Govinda.

"Once Indra, the King of heaven, surrounded by the demigods approached the Supreme Lord and prayed to Him as follows. 'O Lord of the universe, O Supreme Personality of Godhead, we offer our respectful obeisances to You. You are the supreme shelter, the mother and father of everyone. You create, maintain and destroy everyone. You are the benefactor of the earth, the sky, and the entire material creation. You Yourself are Lord Brahmā, Lord Viṣṇu, and Lord Śiva. You are the Lord and enjoyer of all kinds of sacrifices, austerities, hymns and their performers. There is no object within these three animate and inanimate worlds which is not owned and controlled by You. O Lord! O Supreme Personality of Godhead! O master of the demigods! O protector of the surrendered souls! O supreme mystic! The demigods have been deprived of their heavenly kingdom and have been driven out by the demons. They have fearfully surrendered to Your lotus feet. Please protect them. O Lord of the universe! We have fallen from the heavenly planets into this earthly planet and have merged into the ocean of miseries. Kindly be pleased with us.'

"On hearing such a pathetic prayer from Indra, Lord Viṣṇu asked him, 'Who is this invincible demon who has defeated even the demigods? What is his name? What is the source of his prowess? O Indra! Please explain to me everything in detail without any fear.'

"Indra replied, 'O Lord of the demigods! O deliverer of the devotees! O Supreme Lord! A fierce demon named Nadijangha who first caused distress to the demigods, appeared in the family of a *brāhmaṇa*. He had an equally powerful infamous demon son called Mura. The great city of Candravati is the capital of this great demon Mura. This demon Mura has driven out all the demigods from the heavenly planets and he is living there instead. He has taken over the posts of Indra, Agni, Yama, Vayu, Isa, Candrama, Nairita, and Varuna all by himself. All the demigods combined could not conquer him. O Lord Viṣṇu, please kill this demon and protect the demigods.'

"On hearing the words of Indra the Lord became very angry towards those who had harassed the demigods, and said, 'O king of the demigods, I will personally kill this powerful demon who is your enemy. Now all of you should return to the city of Candravati.' Thereafter all the demigods led by Lord Viṣṇu proceeded towards the city of Candravati. On one side the demigods were preparing for the battle with thousands of various weapons in their possession, and on the other side the Demon Mura was roaring, surrounded by an innumerable demon army.

"The demigods were already scattered due to the severe beatings by the demons; but now when the demons saw the rejuvenated fearless demigods led by the Supreme Lord standing before them, the demons became extremely angry. Although the Lord easily defeated all the other demons, He felt difficulty in defeating the demon Mura. When in spite of using various weapons the Lord could not kill the demon Mura, He engaged in wrestling with the demon for ten thousand years. Finally the Lord defeated the demon and left for Badrikāśrama. In Badrikāśrama the Lord entered a beautiful cave called Hemavati and took rest."

The Supreme Lord continued, "O Arjuna! Thereafter that demon chased Me and entered that cave. On seeing Me resting there, he decided to kill Me. At that time an effulgent daughter appeared from My body, and holding various divine weapons began to fight with the demon. After constantly fighting with the demon for a long time, the effulgent goddess finally severed his head. Then, out of fear, all the other demons ran away to Patalaloka." When the Lord got up from His rest He saw the dead body of the demon Mura lying in front of Him and an effulgent goddess humbly standing before Him with folded hands. On seeing her, the Lord asked her in surprise, 'Who are you?'

"The goddess replied, 'O my Lord, I am born from Your body and I have killed this demon. On seeing You lying down, this demon attempted to kill You, therefore I have killed him.'

"The Supreme Lord said, 'O Goddess, I am very pleased with you for this act. You can ask for any benediction you desire.' When the goddess prayed for a benediction the Lord said, ' You are My spiritual energy and since you have appeared on the day of Ekādaśī your name will be Ekādaśī. Anyone who will follow the vow of Ekādaśī will be relieved from all sinful reactions and attain inexhaustible heavenly happiness.'

"From that day onwards the day of Ekādaśī has been nourished and worshiped in this world. O Arjuna, I award the supreme destination to a person who observes the vow of Ekādaśī. O son of Kunti, an Ekādaśī mixed with Dvādaśī is the highest. One should give up sex life, eating grains, honey, meat, eating on a bell metal plate, and applying oil on the day of Ekādaśī. If a person observes this Ekādaśī and hears its glories he can attain even more results.

Chapter 2

Mokṣadā Ekādaśī

This Mokṣadā Ekādaśī occurs during the waxing moon in the month of November/December. The glories of this Ekādaśī are described in *Brahmāṇḍa Purāṇa* in the conversation between Lord Kṛṣṇa and Mahārāja Yudhiṣṭhira.

Once Yudhiṣṭhira asked Lord Kṛṣṇa, "My dear Kṛṣṇa, what is the name of the Ekādaśī that occurs during the waxing moon in the month of November/December? Also please explain to me in details about the procedure for observing this Ekādaśī."

Lord Kṛṣṇa said, "O best of kings! This Ekādaśī destroys all one's sinful reactions. If one worships the Supreme Lord with *tulasī mañjarīs* on this day, the Lord becomes extremely pleased. By observing this Ekādaśī one achieves the result of performing Vajpeya sacrifice."

"There was a king named Vaikānasa who lived and ruled in the city of Campaka. The King was very affectionate towards the citizens. Many qualified *brāhmaṇas* who were well versed in Vedic knowledge lived in his kingdom. One day the King had a dream that his father had fallen in the hell and was suffering unlimited miseries there. On seeing this, the King became struck with wonder. The next day the King disclosed the topics of his dream in an assembly of learned *brāhmaṇas*. He also informed them that his father has requested him to deliver him from the hellish condition. Ever since the King had this dream he became restless, and did not feel any happiness or interest in ruling his kingdom. He even dealt with his family members indifferently. He thought that the life, kingdom, opulence, power, and influence of a son is completely useless if his father is suffering in hell. Therefore the King pathetically appealed to all the learned *brāhmaṇas*, 'Please tell me the way by which I can deliver my father from the clutches of hell.'

On hearing his appeal the *brāhmaṇas* said, 'O King, the *āśrama* of Parvata Muni is situated a short distance from here. He is the knower of past, present and future. You please relate the topics of your dream to him.'

"After hearing their suggestion, King Vaikānasa, accompanied by the *brāhmaṇas* and his subjects, went to the *āśrama* of Parvata Muni. When Parvata Muni inquired about the well-being of his kingdom, King Vaikānasa said, 'O my Lord, we are all very well by your mercy, but in spite of possessing the kingdom and all opulences I am in great difficulty. In fact, a doubt has arisen in my mind and in order to remove that I have come to your lotus feet.'

"After hearing the whole incident from the King, Parvata Muni sat down in deep meditation. After a while he got up from his meditation and said to the King, 'My dear King, your father was very lusty in his previous life, hence he has degraded himself to this condition. Now you all should observe the vow of Ekādaśī which occurs during the waxing moon in the month of November/December for the deliverance of your father and donate the accumulated piety to him. Then by the influence of that piety your father will be relieved from the clutches of hellish life.' After hearing these words from Parvata Muni, the King returned to his palace, surrounded by his entourage.

"Thereafter in due course of time the King with his wife, children, and servants duly observed this Ekādaśī which occurs during the waxing moon in the month of November/December, and dedicated all its piety to his suffering father. By the influence of this piety the father attained the heavenly planet and blessed his son very much.

"O King, one who properly follows this Mokṣadā Ekādaśī is certainly relieved from all sinful reactions."

Chapter 3

Saphalā Ekādaśī

This Saphalā Ekādaśī occurs during the waning moon in the month of December/January. The glories of this Ekādaśī are described in the *Brahmāṇḍa Purāṇa* in the conversation between Lord Kṛṣṇa and Mahārāja Yudhiṣṭhira.

Mahārāja Yudhiṣṭhira said, "O Kṛṣṇa, what is the name of the Ekādaśī that occurs during the waning moon in the month of December/January, and how should one observed it? Please explain this to me in detail."

The Supreme Lord Śrī Kṛṣṇa replied, "O best of the Bharata Dynasty, just as Sesa is best among the snakes, Garuḍa is best among the birds, the horse sacrifice is best among the sacrifices, the Ganges is best among the rivers, Lord Viṣṇu is best among the demigods and the *brāhmaṇas* are best among the human beings, similarly among all the vows the day of Ekādaśī is best. O best of kings, anyone who observes Ekādaśī is very dear to Me. The amount of piety one accumulates by undergoing austerities for five thousand years, is achieved simply by observing Ekādaśī."

There was a famous king named Mahismata who lived in the city of Champavati. This King had four sons. Among them, the eldest son named Lumpaka was very sinful. He used to blaspheme the *brāhmaṇas*, Vaiṣṇavas and the demigods and was extremely attached to gambling and prostitution. Consequently his father, King Mahismata, exiled him. The exiled Lumpaka lived in the jungle and at night began to plunder wealth from the people of his father's kingdom. In spite of his stealing, the citizens would set him free knowing him to be the son of the King. Lumpaka spent his life by regularly eating raw meats and fruits.

There was a banyan tree in this forest who was as worshipable as the demigods. Lumpaka lived underneath this tree for some time.

Coincidentally when Lumpaka was living in this way, the Ekādaśī of the waning moon of the month of November-December occurred. Due to fatigue and weakness, he became unconscious on the day before Ekādaśī and regained his consciousness at mid-day on Ekādaśī. Actually there was no possibility of Lumpaka's killing any animal on that day because he was so weak being severely afflicted with hunger. Therefore he found some fruits and offered them to Lord Viṣṇu for His pleasure, and by that time the sun had set. That night Lumpaka remained awake.

As a result of fasting and keeping awake he unknowingly observed Saphalā Ekādaśī. Lord Madhusūdana accepts the worship and vow of this Ekādaśī offered by the practitioner, so, a result of performing this Ekādaśī Lumpaka got an opulent kingdom. On the next morning a divine horse came and stood before Lumpaka; at that time a voice from the sky was heard, 'O Prince, by the mercy of Lord Madhusūdana and by the influence of Saphalā Ekādaśī you will receive a kingdom and rule it without any difficulty. Return to your father and enjoy the kingdom.' In accordance with this instruction Lumpaka returned to his father and accepted the responsibility of ruling the kingdom. Thereafter he got a beautiful wife and good sons. In this way Lumpaka happily ruled this kingdom.

By observing the vow of Saphalā Ekādaśī persons attain fame in this life and liberation in next life. Those who follow this Ekādaśī are glorious. By following this Ekādaśī one attains the result of performing an Aśvamedha sacrifice.

Chapter 4

Putradā Ekādaśī

The glories of Putradā Ekādaśī which occurs during the waxing moon in the month of December/January are described in the *Bhaviṣyottara Purāṇa* in the conversation between Lord Kṛṣṇa and Mahārāja Yudhiṣṭhira.

Lord Kṛṣṇa said to Yudhiṣṭhira, "My dear King, the Ekādaśī which occurs during the waxing moon in the month of December/January is called Putradā. By observing this Ekādaśī all one's sinful reactions are counteracted. People become learned and famous by following this Ekādaśī. Now please hear the glories of this auspicious Ekādaśī.

"There was a city named Bhadravati, and a king named Suketumana was ruling. The name of his queen was Saivya. Since they had no son both the King and Queen lived their lives in distress. They spent most of their time performing religious activities. Because the King and the Queen were afflicted with lamentation, the water that they offered during the time of offering oblation to their forefathers appeared hot. Meanwhile, the forefathers were also worried, thinking that after King Suketumana no one would be there to offer them oblations. Knowing this distress of the forefathers, the King became even more morose, and did not feel any pleasure in the association of his friends, well-wishers or ministers. Being merged in lamentation and hopelessness, the King considered that without a son human life is useless. It is impossible to become free from the debts to the demigods, to the forefathers and to the human beings without possessing a son. Without heaps of pious activities and devotion to Viṣṇu, one cannot possess sons, wealth and knowledge. After concluding in this way, for his own benefit the morose King secretly left for the forest riding on a horse.

"King Suketumana entered the forest which was inhabited by birds and beasts and began to search for a place to take rest. Within the dense forest the King saw various trees such as Banyan,

Pipala, Date, Tamarind, Palm, Shal, Maulasiri, Saptaparna, Tilaka, Tamala, Sarala, Hingoṭa, Arjuna, Lavhera, Baheda, Sallaki, Patala, Catechu and Palasa as well as various animals such as tigers, lions, wild elephant, deer, wild pigs, monkeys, snakes, leopards and hares. Instead of resting, the King then began to wander through the forest. The King became scared and surprised by hearing the howling of the jackals, and the sounds of the owls. Wandering in this way in all directions the King soon became very tired. It was midday and the King was very thirsty. He thought that though I have pleased the demigods through worship and sacrifices, maintained my subjects like my own children and satisfied the *brāhmaṇas* by offering them foodstuffs and *dakṣiṇa*, still I am suffering like this today. Being absorbed in this thought King Suketumana wandered here and there. Suddenly He saw a lake which was as beautiful as Manasa sarovara filled with lotuses. Many swans, chakravaka and cakora birds were sporting in the waters of that lake. On seeing some sages chanting Vedic mantras on the bank of this lake, the King got down from his horse and offered obeisances to each of them separately. The sages became pleased by the King's behavior and asked him, 'O King. We are pleased with you. Please ask us for some benediction.'

"The King said, 'Who are all of you? Why have you come to this lake?' The sages replied, 'We are Visva devas, and have come here to take bath. Today is the auspicious Putradā Ekādaśī. If a person desirous of a son observes this vow, he is certainly benedicted with a son.' The king said, 'I have tried so many things to get a son, but till today I have not been successful. Since all of you are pleased with me kindly bless me with a beautiful son.' Then the sages instructed, 'Today is Putradā Ekādaśī, O King, observe this Ekādaśī with great care; then by the mercy of the Lord and by our blessing, you will certainly receive a son.'

"Thereafter, following the instruction of the sages the King observed the auspicious Putradā Ekādaśī. On the next day he broke his fast and after repeatedly offering obeisances to the sages, he returned to his palace.

"In due course of time Queen Saivya became pregnant. By the blessings of the sages and the influence of the piety accumulated by observing Putradā Ekādaśī, the King begot a pious and brilliant son. Thereafter the King happily ruled his kingdom, and his forefathers also became satisfied."

Lord Kṛṣṇa continued, "O King Yudhiṣṭhira, by following this Putradā Ekādaśī one can get a son and attain the heavenly planets."

Anyone who hears or sings the glories of this Ekādaśī certainly achieves the results of an Asvamedha sacrifice.

Chapter 5

Ṣaṭ-tilā Ekādaśī

This Ekādaśī occurs during the waning moon in the month of January/February. The glories of Ṣaṭ-tilā Ekādaśī are described in the *Bhaviṣyottara Purāṇa*. Once the sage Dalbhya asked sage Pulastya, "O respected *brāhmaṇa*, people are engaged in various sinful activities such as killing *brāhmaṇas* and in sense gratification in this mortal world. Please explain to me how can they be delivered from this hellish condition which comes as a result of their sinful activities." Sage Pulastya replied, "O most fortunate one! One should worship the Supreme Lord in a pure state of mind on the day of Ekādaśī which occurs during the waning moon in the month of January/February.

"At the time of worship one should pray as follows. O Lord Janārdana! O most merciful Śrī Kṛṣṇa! You are the deliverer of the sinful people. Please be merciful to those who are drowning in the ocean of material existence. O Supreme Brahman! O Supreme Personality of Godhead! O Lord of the universe! Please accept my worship with Your consort Śrīmati Lakṣmīdevi. Thereafter one should worship the *brāhmaṇas* by giving in charity to them umbrellas, cloth, shoes and a pitcher filled with water. According to one's capacity one should also give a black cow and sesame seeds in charity to the best of the *brāhmaṇas*. By giving sesame seeds in charity one can live in the heavenly planets for many, many years.

"One should bath in water mixed with sesame seeds, smear sesame seed paste on his body, perform fire sacrifice with sesame seeds, offer oblations to the forefathers with the water mixed with sesame seeds, eat sesame seeds and give sesame seeds in charity on this Ekādaśī. By doing so all one's sinful reactions will be destroyed. Thus the name of this Ekādaśī is Ṣaṭ-tilā Ekādaśī.'

Lord Kṛṣṇa narrated the following story to Narada Muni when he approached Kṛṣṇa to hear the glories and results of observing Ṣaṭ-tilā Ekādaśī. In the ancient times there lived a female brahmani. She strictly followed the vow of celibacy and engaged in worshiping the Lord. By constantly observing various vows in the course of her worship she gradually became weak and skinny. Although she gave charity to the poor *brāhmaṇas* and unmarried girls, she never pleased the *brāhmaṇas* and demigods by giving food grains in charity. So I considered that although the body of the brahmani became weak from performing many severe vows, still she was a purified soul. Moreover she had not given any food grains in charity to the hungry people. O best of the *brāhmaṇas*! In order to test this brahmani I took the form of a mendicant and personally appeared in this mortal world. I took a begging pot in My hands and approached the house of that brahmani to beg alms.

"The brahmani said, 'O *brāhmaṇa*! Please tell me the truth. Where have you come from?' I pretended to not have heard anything and begged for the alms again. She became angry at this and took a handful of clay and put it in My begging pot. Thereafter I returned to My abode. That ascetic brahmani, as a result of observing severe vows, also returned to My abode. She got a beautiful house, but due to offering Me clay in charity she had no food grains or wealth in her house. O *brāhmaṇa*! When she entered that house she did not find anything and gradually due to lack of wealth she became restless. Thereafter she approached Me in an angry mood and said, ' O Janārdana! I have undergone severe austerities, vows and worshiped Lord Viṣṇu adequately. Why am I bereft of food grains and wealth?'

"Then I said, 'O Brahmani! You have come here from the material world, now please go back to your house. Out of curiosity the wives of the demigods will come to your house for *darśana* and then you should inquire from them about the glories of Ṣaṭ-tilā Ekādaśī. Do not open the door until they finish the narration.' After hearing My statement the brahmani returned home.

"One day when the brahmani was sitting in her room with the door closed from inside some wives of the demigods came there and said, ' O beautiful one! We have come here for *darśana*. Please open the door.' The brahmani replied, ' If you want to see me then please explain to me the importance, piety and glories of Ṣaṭ-tilā Ekādaśī before I open the door.' Then one of the wives of the demigods narrated the glories of this Ekādaśī. After hearing the narration, the brahmani became satisfied and opened the door and the wives of the demigods became pleased by seeing her.

"Under the instruction of these demigoddesses the brahmani observed the vow of Ṣaṭ-tilā Ekādaśī. Thereafter she became beautiful, effulgent and became the proprietor of sufficient food grains, wealth and gold. However no one should observe this Ekādaśī being controlled by greed. By following this Ekādaśī one's misfortune and poverty are destroyed. If one donates sesame seeds on this day then all his sinful reactions are vanquished."

Chapter 6

Jayā Ekādaśī

The glories of Jayā Ekādaśī which occurs during the waxing moon in the month of January/February, are described in the *Bhaviṣyottara Purāṇa* in the conversation between Lord Kṛṣṇa and Mahārāja Yudhiṣṭhira.

Once Mahārāja Yudhiṣṭhira asked Lord Śrī Kṛṣṇa, "O Lord Kṛṣṇa! O original Personality of Godhead, O Lord of the universe Śrī Kṛṣṇa! You are the original cause of the four types of living entities, namely those who are born from perspiration, those born from seeds, those born from eggs and those born from embryos. You alone are the creator, maintainer and destroyer of everything. Please describe to me the glories of that Ekādaśī which occurs during the waxing moon in the month of January/February. Also please explain to me the procedure for observing this Ekādaśī and which deity is to be worshiped on this auspicious day." Lord Kṛṣṇa said, "O best of kings, Yudhiṣṭhira! The Ekādaśī which occurs during the waxing moon in the month of January/February is celebrated as Jayā Ekādaśī. By following this Ekādaśī all one's sinful reactions are vanquished. The performer of this Ekādaśī will never have to accept the body of a ghost. O King! As far as awarding liberation and exhausting one's sinful reactions are concerned, this Ekādaśī has no substitute. O lion-like King! Now please hear the description of this Ekādaśī which I had previously narrated in *Padma Purāṇa*."

"The demigods were living happily in the heavenly kingdom of Indra under his rule. In the Nandan Kanana forest which was filled with the fragrance of fully blossomed Parijata flowers and where the Apsarās freely enjoyed their lives, Indra also enjoyed various exchanges with the Apsarās. Once, being in a pleasant mood, Indra arranged a dance festival of fifty million Apsarās. In that assembly there was a Gandharva singer named Puṣpadanta. Also a Gandharva named Chitrasena came there along with his wife Malini and his daughter. Chitrasena had a son named Puṣpavana whose son was Malyavan. A Gandharvi named Puṣpavatī became attracted by the beauty of Malyavan. Being pierced by the sharp arrows of cupid, the most beautiful Puṣpavatī tried various ways, such as by gestures and glances, to bring Malyavan under her control. O King! How can I describe the splendid beauty of Puṣpavatī? She had beautiful arms which resembled the ropes of cupid, and the beauty of her face resembled the full moon. She had broad eyes, ears decorated with ear rings, and her neck defeated the beauty of the conch. Her waist was thin, her breasts were highly raised, her hips were broad and her thighs were like banana trees. Her shining feet defeated the beauty of the red lotus flower. All her beautiful features appeared even more enchanting because of being decorated with gorgeous ornaments and garments. On seeing such a beautiful woman as Puṣpavatī, Malyavan became totally captivated.

"In order to please Indra, both Malyavan and Puṣpavatī began to perform dancing and singing with other Apsarās in that dance festival. But since they were attracted to each other they could not perform well. As a result there was a disturbance in the ongoing performance of the dancing assembly. Continuously looking at each other through the corners of their eyes they became pierced by the arrows of Cupid. When Indra noticed the perpetual disturbance in the process of singing and dancing he understood their mental condition. Due to the constant disturbance in their performance Indra felt insulted and cursed them as follows. ' Both of you are fools and sinful. You have disobeyed my order, hence I am cursing you. Both of you will accept the bodies of a male and female ghost and take birth in the earthly planet and enjoy the result of your karma.'

"After being cursed in this way both Malyavan and Puṣpavatī received the bodies of a ghost and began to spend their miserable lives within a cave of the Himalaya Mountain. As a result of receiving ghost bodies both of them felt great distress and lamentation. By the influence of the curse they could not take pleasure from the sense of smelling, touch or sleeping. While wandering in the dense forest and cold mountainous regions of Himalaya, they sat down somewhere and began to introspect. The male ghost said to the female ghost, ' Alas, what heinous sinful activities we have committed that we have received such a miserable ghost body.' Feeling extreme sadness they merged into the ocean of repentance. Both Malyavan and Puṣpavatī, in the form of male and female ghosts spent that whole day without taking any food while continuously repenting for their misdeeds. Co-incidentally this day was the auspicious day of Jayā Ekādaśī which occurs during the waxing moon in the month of January/February. Although they were extremely afflicted with hunger and thirst, they did not kill any living entity on that day. They even abstained from taking any roots, fruits or water. O King! In this way, when the ghost couple was sitting underneath the banyan tree in a miserable condition, the sun was about to set. Due to the freezing cold and being absorbed in deep thought they felt great unhappiness and spend that entire night without sleeping. Due to their mental disturbance no propensity for sense gratification appeared in their hearts.

"O lion-hearted King! In this way they unknowingly observed the vow of Jayā Ekādaśī, and by the influence of the piety accumulated from observing this vow the very next day they attained liberation from their ghost bodies. Thereafter Puṣpavatī and Malyavan regained their original positions and returned to heaven through air planes. On returning to heaven, they both happily approached Indra, the King of the demigods, and offered their obeisances. When Indra saw them He was struck with wonder and he exclaimed, "What a wonder! By the influence of which piety have your ghostly conditions been destroyed? Which demigod has freed you from my curse?" In answer to this Malyavan said, ' By the causeless mercy of the Supreme Lord and as a result of observing the vow of Jayā Ekādaśī, which is very dear to Him, we have become freed from the curse. O master! I am telling you with full conviction that we have been freed from our ghostly lives simply by the influence of devotional service.'

"After hearing these words, Indra again said to Malyavan, ' You have become purified as a result of executing devotional service to Lord Viṣṇu and observing the vow of Ekādaśī. Therefore now you are worshipable by me also. Those human beings who are engaged in devotional service of Viṣṇu are certainly worshiped and respected by me.' Thereafter Puṣpavatī and Malyavan began to live happily in the heavenly planet.

"O King Yudhiṣṭhira! One must observe the vow of Ekādaśī. Observance of the vow of Jayā Ekādaśī takes away even the sin of killing a *brāhmaṇa*. The secondary fruits of observing this vow is that one automatically receives the piety of giving in charity, performing sacrifice and visiting holy places. If one properly follows the vow of this Ekādaśī with faith and devotion then he lives in Vaikuṇṭha forever.

Just by reading and hearing the glories of this Ekādaśī one can attain the result of an Agnistoma sacrifice.

Chapter 7

Vijayā Ekādaśī

The glories of this Ekādaśī are described in the *Skanda Purāṇa*. Once Mahārāja Yudhiṣṭhira enquired from Śrī Kṛṣṇa, "O Lord Krishna, please be kind to me and describe the Ekādaśī that occurs during the waning moon in the month of February/March."

Lord Kṛṣṇa replied, "O King Yudhiṣṭhira! I will happily describe the Ekādaśī known as Vijayā Ekādaśī to you. By observing the vow of this Ekādaśī all of one's sinful reactions are simultaneously eradicated.

"Once the great sage Nārada asked Lord Brahmā, 'O best of the demigods! Kindly described to me the result one achieves by following the vow of Vijayā Ekādaśī which occurs during the waning moon in the month of February/March.' In reply to this, Lord Brahmā said,' My dear son, this oldest vow is pure and is the destroyer of all sinful activities. Actually it gives great results, as its name suggests. This Vijayā Ekādaśī undoubtedly awards one the power of victory. When Śrī Rāmacandra went to the forest for fourteen years with His wife Sitadevi and brother Lakṣmaṇa in order to fulfill the order of His father, They lived in a beautiful forest known as Panchavati on the bank of the river Godavari for some time. While residing in this forest, one day Rāvaṇa, the King of demons, kidnapped austere Sitadevi. Due to separation from Sitadevi, Rāmacandra became overwhelmed with extreme distress. While wandering throughout the forest in search of Sita, Rāmacandra met with Jatayu, the King of the birds, who was about to die. Jatayu told Rāmacandra everything about Sita and then left this world returning to Vaikuṇṭha. Thereafter Rāmacandra made friendship with Sugriva. Many monkey soldiers were gathered to help the mission of Rāmacandra. Meanwhile Hanuman, the King of the monkeys, completed a great mission by going to the Ashoka forest in Lanka, meeting Sitadevi, and convincing Her by giving Rāmacandra's ring to her. Thereafter Hanuman returned to Rāmacandra and explained the whole incident to Him. After hearing the words of Hanuman, Rāmacandra had a meeting with His friend Sugriva and resolved to invade Lanka. Rāmacandra gathered a great number of monkey soldiers and arrived at the shore of the ocean. He then said to Lakṣmaṇa, 'O Saumitra! How will We cross beyond this unfathomable ocean which is full of fierce aquatics such as whales and crocodiles?' Lakṣmaṇa replied, 'O original Supreme Personality of Godhead! You are the primeval Lord. There is a great sage named Bakadalbhya who lives in this island. His *āśrama* is situated four miles away from here. O son of the dynasty of Raghu! This sage has had *darśana* of Lord Brahmā. We should ask him about the means of crossing this ocean.' Being advised by Lakṣmaṇa in this way, Lord Rāmacandra went to the *āśrama* of Bakadalbhya and offered respectful obeisances to him. The omniscient sage could immediately understand that this personality was the Supreme Lord Rāmacandra and that for some particular cause, such as killing the demon Rāvaṇa, He has now appeared in this material world. The great sage asked him,' O Rāmacandra, for what purpose You have kindly come here?' Rāmacandra replied, 'O *brāhmaṇa*! by your mercy I have come here on the shore of this ocean with my soldiers in order to fight the demons and conquer Lanka. O best of the sages! Please tell me a simple method by which I can easily cross over this insurmountable ocean. Only for this reason I have come to your lotus feet.'

"The great sage said to Rāmacandra, 'O Rāmacandra! I will tell You about observing a great vow by which You will certainly conquer Your battle and obtain extraordinary fame and opulence in this world. However, You should follow this vow with undeviated attention. O Rāma! There is an Ekādaśī known as Vijayā which occurs during the waning moon in the month of February/March. By observing this Ekādaśī You will certainly be able to cross over this ocean with Your monkey soldiers. O Lord Rāmacandra! Now please hear about the procedure for following this Ekādaśī. On the day before Ekādaśī You should fill either a golden, silver, copper or clay pitcher with water and decorate it with mango twigs. Then You should place this pitcher on a sanctified raised altar which is decorated with seven kinds of grains. Then You should place a golden deity of Lord Nārāyaṇa upon this pitcher. On the day of Ekādaśī You should take bath early in the morning and worship this deity of Lord Nārāyaṇa with devotion by offering various items such as Tulasi leaves, sandalwood paste, flowers, garlands, incense, a ghee lamp and foodstuff. You should also remain awake that night. On the day after Ekādaśī You should place this pitcher on the bank of a river, pond or lake after the sunrise and duly worship it. Thereafter You should donate this pitcher, along with the deity of Nārāyaṇa, to a *brāhmaṇa* who strictly follows the vow of celibacy. By doing so you will certainly conquer over Your enemies.'

"According to the instruction of this great sage, Lord Rāmacandra exhibited the ideal example of properly following this vow of Ekādaśī, and consequently He was victorious. A person who properly follows this vow of Ekādaśī certainly becomes victorious in this life and in the next. Lord Brahmā continued to speak to Nārada, ' O my dear son! Therefore every human being should follow the vow of this Vijayā Ekādaśī. The glories of Vijayā Ekādaśī destroy all one's sinful reactions.

"One who reads or hears the glories of this Ekādaśī obtains the result of a Vajapayee sacrifice."

Chapter 8

Āmalakī Ekādaśī

The topics of the glories of Āmalakī Ekādaśī which occurs during the waxing moon in the month of February/March are described in the *Brahmāṇḍa Purāṇa* in the conversation between King Mandhata and sage Vasiṣṭha.

Once King Mandhata asked the sage Vasiṣṭha, "O most fortunate one if you are pleased with and merciful to me then kindly describe to me about a vow by following of which I can attain all auspiciousness." The sage Vasiṣṭha replied, "O King, now I will explain to you the glories and history of a great vow which awards one all auspiciousness. O King! The name of this vow is Āmalakī Ekādaśī. The influence of the piety accumulated by following this Ekādaśī certainly destroys all one's sinful reactions and awards liberation as well as the result of donating one thousand cows in charity.

"In the ancient times there was a city named Vaidisa that was inhabited by many healthy and prosperous *brāhmaṇas*, *kṣatriyas*, *vaiśyas* and *śūdras*. O lion-hearted King, there was no atheistic or sinful person in this beautiful city. The entire city was filled with the sound of Vedic mantras. In this famous city there lived a truthful pious king named Caitraratha who was born in the family of King Pasabinduka, a member of the dynasty of the moon. King Caitraratha was powerful, heroic, opulent and well versed in the scriptures. During the reign of this king all auspiciousness and prosperity was found in the kingdom. All his subjects were attached to the devotional service of Lord Viṣṇu and all of them observed the vow of Ekādaśī. Due to remaining engaged in the devotional service of Lord Hari everyone lived happily in his kingdom. There was not a single poor or miserly person in his kingdom. After living happily for many many years in this way once Āmalakī Ekādaśī conjoined with Dvādaśī which occurs during the waxing moon in the month of February/March. Realizing that this Ekādaśī bestows great benefits, the King and his subjects resolved to observe this Ekādaśī with proper rules and regulations. Early in the morning on the day of Ekādaśī the King and his subjects took bath in the river and went to the temple of Lord Viṣṇu which was situated on the river bank. Within the temple there was an *āmalakī* tree where the King placed a pitcher filled with water and an umbrella, cloths, shoes and five kinds of jewels for the worship. Thereafter the King worshiped Lord Parasurama and *āmalakī* by offering water, shoes, canopy, gold, diamonds, rubies, pearls, sapphires and fragrant incense. Then the King, led by the sages and followed by his subjects, offered prayers to Lord Parasurama as follows. 'O Lord Parasurama! O Son of Renuka! O You who is situated under the shade of the *āmalakī* tree! O bestower of material enjoyment and liberation, I offer my respectful obeisances to You.' Then they offered prayers to the *āmalakī* tree. 'O *āmalakī*! O Sustainer of the Universe! O Offspring of Lord Brahmā! O destroyer of all sins! We offer our respectful obeisances to you. Kindly accept our offering.' After properly worshiping the Lord and *āmalakī* in this way, the King, accompanied by his subjects remained awake that night within the temple of Lord Viṣṇu. They sang songs and offered beautiful prayers with devotion in praise of the Lord and the *āmalakī* tree. At that time, by the arrangement of Providence, a hunter came there. This hunter earned his livelihood simply by killing various living entities. When he came to the temple which was decorated with a ghee lamp, incense and other auspicious items and saw that many people were remaining awake while glorifying the Lord, he sat down with them and began to contemplate what was going on? The fortunate hunter took *darśana* of Lord Dāmodara who was placed on the top of the pitcher and began to hear the transcendental topics of Viṣṇu. Although he was afflicted with hunger he was astonished to see this and remained awake that whole night while hearing the glories of Ekādaśī. In the morning the King left for his palace accompanied by his subjects. The hunter also returned home and happily took his meal. After many, many years the hunter left his body. By the influence of Āmalakī Ekādaśī and as a result of remaining awake on the night of this Ekādaśī in his next life the hunter became a king with innumerable elephants, horses, chariots and a large army. The hunter took birth as Vasurath the powerful son of King Vidurath who ruled the famous city of Jayanti. King Vasurath ruled one million villages. He was as brilliant as the sun, as effulgent as the moon as powerful as Lord Viṣṇu, and as tolerant as the earth. He was truthful and fixed in his occupational duties and thus became a great devotee of Lord Viṣṇu.

"One day King Vasurath, who was very kind and charitable, lost his way while hunting in the forest. He was extremely tired and afflicted with hunger. Not finding any other alternative the King lied down within that dense forest using his arm as a pillow. At that time some mlecchas who lived in that forest came before the sleeping king and began to torture him in various ways. Considering the King to be their enemy, they attempted to kill him. They thought that this king had previously killed our fathers, mothers, sons, grandsons and uncles and has compelled us to wander aimlessly. Speaking in this way the mlecchas took up their different weapons and began to beat the King. But to their utter surprise, none of their weapons touched the body of the King, and as a result the King did not feel any injury at all. When all their weapons were used up the mlecchas became morose and lifeless due to fear. They lost all power to move any further. At that time a beautiful extraordinary woman decorated with various ornaments and fragrant sandalwood paste appeared from the body of the King. She was decorated with an attractive flower garland and her eyes were reddish due to anger. She raised her eye brow, and holding a disc in her hand she rushed towards the mlecchas to kill them in an angry mood. Within a moment that powerful woman killed all the sinful mlecchas. After this incident, the King woke up. On seeing such a ghastly scene the King, who just got up from sleep, became frightened and stunned. When the King saw his fierce looking enemies lying killed he became astonished and said, 'Alas! Who is that most well-wishing friend of mine who has protected my life by killing these powerful enemies? I convey my heartfelt gratitude to him for this great act.' At that time a voice from the sky was heard, 'Who else except Lord Keśava is capable of protecting His surrendered souls? He alone is the maintainer of surrendered devotees.' After hearing this voice from the sky, the King became extremely amazed and his heart melted with devotional feeling. Thereafter the King returned to his palace and ruled his kingdom just like Indra, without any obstacles."

The Sage Vasiṣṭha continued, "My dear King! Any person who observes the vow of this sacred Āmalakī Ekādaśī undoubtedly returns to the abode of Lord Viṣṇu."

Chapter 9

Pāpamocanī Ekādaśī

The glories of Pāpamocanī Ekādaśī are described in the *Bhaviṣyottara Purāṇa* in the conversation between Lord Kṛṣṇa and Mahārāja Yudhiṣṭhira.

Once Mahārāja Yudhiṣṭhira asked Lord Kṛṣṇa, "My dear Lord Kṛṣṇa, You have already explained the glories of Āmalakī Ekādaśī. Now please describe the Ekādaśī which occurs during the waning moon in the month of March/April. What is the name of this Ekādaśī? Also describe to me the procedure for observing this Ekādaśī and its results." Lord Kṛṣṇa replied, "O best of Kings! The name of this Ekādaśī is Pāpamocanī. Now please hear its glories as I describe them to you. Long, long ago the glories of this Ekādaśī were spoken by the Sage Lomaśa to King Mandata. This Pāpamocanī Ekādaśī occurs during the waning moon in the month of March/April. This Ekādaśī takes away all one's sinful reactions, destroys one's ghostly condition of life and awards eight kinds of mystic perfections."

"Sage Lomaśa said, ' In the ancient time Kuvera, the treasurer of the demigods, had a beautiful forest of flowers called Caitraratha where the weather was pleasant as a result of an eternal spring. The heavenly dancing girls, such as the Gandharvas and Kinnaras, enjoyed various sports there. Demigods headed by Indra used to come there and enjoy various exchanges. In that forest a great sage named Medhāvī who was a staunch devotee of Lord Śiva was engaged in performing austerity. The Apsarās, or the heavenly dancing girls tried to disturb the sage in various ways. Among the Apsarās one famous Apsarā named Mañju Ghoṣā devised a means to captivate the mind of the sage. Due to fear of the sage, Mañju Ghoṣā built a cottage a little away from the *āśrama* of the sage and began to sing in a sweet voice accompanied with the musical instrument Bina. On seeing Mañju Ghoṣā, who applied sandal wood pulp on her body, wore a fragrant flower garland and was engaged in singing sweetly, even the cupid who is an enemy of Lord Śiva tried to conquer the sage who was the devotee of Lord Śiva. One time Lord Siva burnt the cupid to ashes, thus remembering his previous enmity, cupid entered the body of the sage in order to take revenge . At that time sage Medhāvī, who wore a white sacred thread on his body and who lived in the *āśrama* of Cyavana Rsi, appeared as the second cupid. The lusty Mañju Ghoṣā slowly came before the sage. The sage Medhāvī also became overwhelmed by lust and forgot his worshipable Lord. He gave up the practice of devotional service and became so intoxicated in relishing the association of this woman that he even lost the sense of discriminating between day and night. In this way sage Medhāvī spend many years enjoying lusty activities.

Thereafter, when Mañju Ghoṣā saw that the sage has fallen down from his position, she decided to return to the heavenly planet. She said to sage Medhāvī who was engaged in conjugal affair, 'O great sage! Now please give me permission to return home.' Then sage Medhāvī replied, 'O beautiful woman! You have come to me only in the evening. Stay here tonight and you can return in the morning.' On hearing these words of the sage, Mañju Ghoṣā became frightened and continued to live with him for a few more years. In this way, although Mañju Ghoṣā lived with the sage for fifty-seven years, nine months and three days, still it appeared to be only half of a night to the sage. Mañju Ghoṣā again asked for permission from the sage to return home but the sage said, 'O beautiful one! Please hear my words. This is only morning. Please wait till I finish my morning rituals.' Then the Apsarā smiled and said to the sage with amazement, 'O great sage! How long will it take to complete your morning rituals? Haven't you finished yet? You have spent many years enjoying my association. Therefore please consider the actual value of the time.' On hearing the words of the Apsarā, the sage came to his senses and after carefully calculating the time he said, 'Alas! O beautiful one! I have simply wasted fifty-seven years of my valuable time. You have ruined everything and spoiled all my austerities.' The eyes of the sage filled with tears and his entire body began to tremble. Sage Medhāvī cursed Mañju Ghoṣā in the following words, 'You have behaved with me like a witch. Therefore you will immediately become a witch. O sinful unchaste Lady! Shame on you.'

"After being cursed by the sage in this way Mañju Ghoṣā humbly said to the sage, 'O best of the *brāhmaṇas*! Please withdraw your heavy curse. I have spent many years in your company. O my Lord, for this reason I am a fit candidate for your forgiveness. Please be merciful to me.' The sage replied, 'O gentle lady! What will I do now ? You have destroyed my entire wealth of austerity. Still, I am telling you the procedure for getting free from this curse. The Ekādaśī which occurs during the waning moon in the month of March/April which is called Pāpamocanī and is capable of destroying all one's sinful reactions, if you follow this Ekādaśī strictly and faithfully then your ghostly condition of life will be vanquished.' After speaking these words, sage Medhāvī returned to the *āśrama* of his father, sage Cyavana. As soon as sage Cyavana saw his fallen son he became extremely unhappy and said, 'Alas! Alas! O my son what have you done? You have ruined yourself. You should not have spoiled your entire treasury of austerity simply by being captivated by an ordinary lady.' Sage Medhāvī replied, 'O respected father! Due to misfortune I have committed great sins in the association of an Apsarā. Therefore please instruct me regarding the atonement of my sinful reactions.' On hearing the pathetic words of his repentant son sage Cyavana said, 'O my son! By observing Pāpamocanī Ekādaśī, which falls during the waning moon in the month of March/April, all one's sinful reactions are completely destroyed. Therefore you should observe this Ekādaśī.' On hearing these kind words of his father, sage Medhāvī exhibited special enthusiasm in observing this Ekādaśī. By the influence of this Ekādaśī all the sinful reactions of sage Medhāvī were destroyed and he became very pious. Meanwhile, Mañju Ghoṣā also observed this auspicious Pāpamocanī Ekādaśī and became liberated from the ghostly condition of life. She then regained her divine form and returned to heaven.

After narrating this story to king Mandata, sage Lomosa concluded as follows. " My dear King, just by observing this Pāpamocanī Ekādaśī all one's sinful reactions are automatically destroyed. By hearing or reading the glories of this Ekādaśī one achieves the result of donating one thousand cows. By observing this Ekādaśī all kinds of sinful reactions resulting from the killing of a *brāhmaṇa*, killing an embryo, drinking wine and associating with one's guru's wife are totally uprooted."

The purport is that since this sacred Ekādaśī is all-auspicious and is the destroyer of all sins, everyone should strictly observe this Ekādaśī.

Chapter 10

Kāmadā Ekādaśī

The glories of Kāmadā Ekādaśī are described in the *Varāha Purāṇa* in the conversation between Lord Kṛṣṇa and Mahārāja Yudhiṣṭhira.

Once Mahārāja Yudhiṣṭhira asked Lord Kṛṣṇa, the crown of the Yadu dynasty, "O Lord Vāsudeva! Please accept my humble obeisances. O my Lord! Please describe to me the Ekādaśī that occurs during the waxing moon in the month of March/April. Also explain to me the procedure for observing this Ekādaśī and what its benefits are."

Lord Kṛṣṇa replied, "My dear Mahārāja Yudhiṣṭhira, please hear attentively the description of this Ekādaśī which is recorded in the *Purāṇa*. One time Mahārāja Dilip, the great grandfather of Lord Rāmacandra, asked his spiritual master, sage Vasiṣṭha, about the name and procedure for observing the Ekādaśī that occurs during the waxing moon in the month of March/April.

"Sage Vasiṣṭha replied, 'O King! I will certainly fulfill your desire. The name of this Ekādaśī is Kāmadā. This sacred Ekādaśī burns all one's sinful reactions to ashes and awards the observer the privilege of having a son. Now please hear its glories from me.

"'Long, long ago there was a city named Ratnapur (Bhogipur). This opulent city was ruled by a king named Puṇḍarīka. He was accompanied by his subjects which included the Gandharvas, Kinnaras and the Apsarās. In that city a beautiful Apsarā named Lalitā and a handsome Gandharva named Lalit lived as husband and wife. They were overwhelmed by each other's love and constantly remained engaged in various sporting activities at their opulent house. The love in Lalitā's heart for her husband, and the love in Lalit's heart for his wife was so intense that they were unable to tolerate even a movement's separation from each other.

"'One time in the court of King Puṇḍarīka many Gandharvas were singing and dancing, and Lalit also sang with them without his wife. Due to the absence of Lalitā, Lalit's voice, tune, steps and wordings became faulty. In the audience there was a snake named Karkotaka who knew about this mystery, so he complained to King Puṇḍarīka about the actual truth of Lalit's behavior. Then the King became extremely angry and cursed Lalit as follows, 'O sinful one! O fool! Being controlled by the lust of your wife you have disturbed the singing and dancing performance. So I curse you to become a man-eater cannibal.'

"'Being cursed by King Puṇḍarīka, Lalit immediately transformed into a great demon. When Lalitā saw her husband's unbelievable and fierce-looking form she became extremely hurt. With intense distress she spent her days and nights simply thinking what to do and where to go. Giving up all embarrassment, she lived with her husband in the forest.

"'Once while wandering within the dense forest with her husband, Lalitā saw the most sacred *āśrama* of the sage Śrīngi situated at the peak of the Vindhya Mountain. Lalitā immediately went there and offered her respectful obeisances to the sage. Upon seeing this lady, the sage inquired, 'O beautiful one, who are you? Whose daughter are you? Why have you come here?' Lalitā replied, 'O great soul, I am the daughter of the Gandharva named Viradhanva. My name is Lalitā. I have come here with my cursed husband. O great sage! My husband has become a demon by the curse of the Gandharva King Puṇḍarīka. O *brāhmaṇa*! I am greatly distressed by seeing his terrible and ferocious form. O my Lord! Kindly explain to me the process of atonement by which my husband can become liberated from the curse. O best of the *brāhmaṇas*! Please instruct us in such a way that his demoniac condition of life is removed.' After hearing Lalitā's pathetic request, the great sage Śrīngi said, 'O daughter of the Gandharva! In a few days' time an Ekādaśī named Kāmadā which occurs during the waxing moon in the month of March/April will approach. By strictly following the vow of this Ekādaśī all one's desires are fulfilled. O gentle lady! According to my instruction you should observe this vow of Ekādaśī and give the entire merit which you have earned by observing this vow to your husband. Then by the influence of this merit your husband will immediately become freed from the curse.'

"O King! Being instructed in this way by the sage, Lalitā gladly observed the vow of this Ekādaśī. On the day of Dvādaśī, Lalitā sat in front of the *brāhmaṇas* and the Supreme Lord Vāsudeva and declared, 'I have observed the vow of Kāmadā Ekādaśī to relieve my husband from the curse. Now by the influence of my earned piety let my husband be freed from the demoniac condition of life.' At that time her husband-turned-demon Lalit was present there. As soon as Lalitā finished her prayer her demon husband became freed from 'l sins and regained his divine Gandharva form. From that time Lalit and Lalitā lived happily together."

Lord Kṛṣṇa continued, "O Mahārāja Yudhiṣṭhira! O best of kings! Anyone who hears this wonderful narration of Kāmadā Ekādaśī should certainly observe it to the best of his ability. There is no better vow of Ekādaśī then this Kāmadā Ekādaśī, for it can eradicate even the sin of killing a *brāhmaṇa* and can counteract the demoniac curses."

Chapter 11

Varuthinī Ekādaśī

The glories of Varuthinī Ekādaśī which occurs during the waning moon in the month of April/May are described in the *Bhaviṣyottara Purāṇa* in the conversation between Lord Kṛṣṇa and Mahārāja Yudhiṣṭhira.

Once Mahārāja Yudhiṣṭhira said to Śrī Kṛṣṇa, "O Vāsudeva! I offer my humble obeisances to You. Please explain the Ekādaśī which occurs during the waning moon in the month of April/May, including its name, influence and glories."

Lord Kṛṣṇa replied, "My dear King, the name of this Ekādaśī is Varuthinī and it awards one good fortune both in this life and in the next. By following the vow of this Ekādaśī a living entity attains perpetual happiness, diminishes his sinful reactions and becomes greatly fortunate. By observing this vow an unfortunate wife becomes fortunate, a human being attains happiness and prosperity both in this life and in the next, they become free from the cycle of birth and death, all their sinful reactions are nullified and they attain devotional service to the Lord. King Mandata was liberated by properly observing this Ekādaśī. Many kings such as Dhundhumara became liberated by following this Ekādaśī. One can achieve the result of undergoing austerities for ten thousand years simply by observing this Varuthinī Ekādaśī. The amount of piety one accumulates by donating 40 kilos of gold during the solar eclipse in Kurukṣetra is achieved simply by observing this Varuthinī Ekādaśī.

"O best of kings! Donating an elephant is superior to donating a horse. Donating land is superior to donating an elephant and donating sesame seeds is greater than donating land. Donating gold is greater than donating sesame seeds and donating food grains is greater than donating gold. In fact, there is no greater charity than giving food grains in charity. O best of kings! By giving food grains in charity one can satisfy the forefathers, the demigods and all living entities. The learned scholars have ascertained that giving a daughter in charity is equal to giving food grains in charity. The Supreme Lord Himself has compared donating food grains to be equal to donating cows. Moreover, among all kinds of charities giving knowledge to others is the highest type of charity.

"By following Varuthinī Ekādaśī one can attain the results of all charities. A person who earns his livelihood by selling his daughter certainly commits a great sin and is fit to live in hell till the time of final annihilation. Therefore no one should ever accept wealth in exchange for his daughter. O king of kings! A householder who, under the influence of greed, sells his daughter in exchange for money becomes a cat in his next life. But one who decorates his daughter with ornaments according to his own capacity and gives her in charity to a qualified groom, even Citragupta, the chief secretary of Yamarāja, is unable to count his piety. The follower of this Ekādaśī should abstain from eating out of a bell metal pot, eating meat, masura gram, chickpea, spinach, honey, accepting foodstuffs cooked by others, eating more than once, and indulging in sex life from the day before Ekādaśī. He should not indulge in gambling, sleeping, eating betel nuts, brushing his teeth, blaspheming anyone, gossiping, speaking with a sinful person, becoming angry and telling lies on the day of Ekādaśī. On the day after Ekādaśī he should not eat on a plate made of bell metal, eat meat, masura gram, and honey, and he should abstain from speaking lies, doing exercise, laboring hard, eating more then once, indulging in sex life, shaving the head or face, applying oil to the body, and eating foodstuff cooked by others. One should carefully avoid all the above-mentioned prohibitions which destroy the vow of Ekādaśī. Apart from these, some other prohibited measures should be observed not only for the three days but forever. If one observes the vow of Varuthinī Ekādaśī according to these prescribed rules and regulations then all his sinful reactions are eradicated and he attains the supreme destination. One who remains awake on the day of Ekādaśī and worships Lord Janārdana becomes freed from all sins and attains the supreme goal of life. Anyone who hears or reads the glories of this Ekādaśī surely achieves the result of donating one thousand cows, and being freed from all his sinful reactions he attains the abode of Viṣṇu."

Chapter 12

Mohinī Ekādaśī

The glories of Mohinī Ekādaśī, which occurs during the waxing moon in the month of April/May, are described in the *Sūrya Purāṇa*.

Once Mahārāja Yudhiṣṭhira asked Lord Kṛṣṇa, "O Janārdana! What is the name of the Ekādaśī that occurs during the waxing moon in the month of April/May, and what is the process for observing this Ekādaśī? Also what is the merit one obtains by following this Ekādaśī? Please explain all these to me in detail."

Lord Kṛṣṇa replied, "O son of Dharma! Please hear Me attentively as I describe the story that sage Vasiṣṭha once told Lord Rāmacandra.

"One time long ago Lord Rāmacandra said to the great sage Vasiṣṭha, 'O respected sage! I am feeling great distress due to separation from Sita, the daughter of King Janaka. Kindly explain to Me the great vow to follow which will mitigate all one's sinful reactions and distresses.'

"The great sage Vasiṣṭha, who was the spiritual master of Rāmacandra, said, 'My dear Rāma, Your intelligence is sharp and mixed with faith. Moreover, Your question is beneficial for the entire humanity. Just by chanting and remembering Your all-auspicious holy names all living entities can become purified and eligible to achieve all auspiciousness. Still, for the benefit of the ordinary people, I will describe to You about a great vow. O Lord Rāma! The Ekādaśī that occurs during the waxing moon in the month of April/May is famous as Mohinī Ekādaśī and is very auspicious. By following this Ekādaśī all one's sinful reactions, material miseries and a network of illusion are destroyed. Now please hear attentively as I narrate the most pious topics of this Ekādaśī.

"There was a beautiful city named Bhadravati situated on the bank of the sacred river Sarasvatī which was ruled by a king named Dyutimana. O Lord Rāma! This king was born in the dynasty of the moon, and he was tolerant and truthful. There was a pious and prosperous devotee of Lord Viṣṇu named Dhanapāla who also lived in that city. He was a *vaiśya* {mercantile community} by profession. For the benefit of the ordinary people this devotee Dhanapāla built many dharmashalas, or guest houses, schools, temples of Lord Viṣṇu, charitable hospitals, wide roads and market places. He also made arrangements for distributing water and foodstuff, he dug wells for cool drinking water and ponds for clear water, he also built gardens for flowers and fruits. In this way he properly utilized his wealth for the benefit of all and thus successfully demonstrated the true meaning of his name. This pious devotee of Lord Viṣṇu who was always peaceful, a benefactor of others and engaged in devotional service to Viṣṇu had five sons namely Samana, Dyutimana, Medhavi, Sukriti and Dhṛṣṭabuddhi. His son Dhṛṣṭabuddhi was most sinful. He was extremely wicked, ill-natured, always engaged in bad association, and having illicit connection with unchaste women. He was also fond of gambling and drinking wine. He even took pleasure in killing and torturing other living entities. In this way he engaged in all kinds of sinful activities and soon turned into an abominable son of a most pious father and was a disgrace to the family. He never showed respect to the demigods, guests, old forefathers or *brāhmaṇas*. He was constantly engaged in thinking of committing sinful activities and thus lived a contemptible life. The sinful wretch Dhṛṣṭabuddhi misused all his father's wealth in many useless activities. He always ate abominable foodstuff and remained always absorbed in drinking wine. One day on seeing his shameless son walking in the public place while placing his hand on the shoulder of a prostitute, Dhanapāla became extremely hurt. On that very day he threw out his spoiled son from the house. Dhṛṣṭabuddhi then became bereft of everyone's affection including from his father, mother, brothers, relatives, and friends. He was degraded from his position in caste society and the pious community and became an object of hatred for everyone.

"After being thrown out from his father's house, Dhṛṣṭabuddhi continued his sinful propensities with the money he received by selling his personal clothes and ornaments. Soon that also came to an end. Gradually, due to lack of sufficient food, his body became weak and skinny. On realizing that he had become poor, his so-called deceitful friends left him, condemning him on various pretexts.

"Dhṛṣṭabuddhi was now full of anxiety. He had no food or clothes and was extremely afflicted with hunger. So he began to contemplate, 'What should I do now? Where should I go? By which means will I survive?' After contemplating in this way, he decided that there was no other alternative than to start stealing for his survival. So with a desire to steal he began to wander throughout the city. Sometimes the King's guard would arrest him and after considering his father's greatness he would release him. After being caught and released in this way many times, he was once again formally arrested for committing a special kind of theft. He was taken to the King who awarded him severe punishment. The King said, 'O sinful foolish creature you cannot stay within this kingdom any more for you are the greatest sinner. I am releasing you for now, but leave this kingdom immediately and go where ever you wish.'

"Dhṛṣṭabuddhi, afraid of being punished again, left the kingdom. He went far away and entered into a dense forest. Within the forest he became so afflicted with hunger and thirst that he began to kill beasts and birds indiscriminately and ate their raw flesh. For many years he wandered throughout the forest like a hunter, holding a bow and arrows in his hands and killing innocent animals and engaging in sinful activities.

"Dhṛṣṭabuddhi was always miserable and anxious, but one day, due to some past pious deeds, he arrived at the sacred *āśrama* of the great sage and ascetic Kauṇḍinya while wandering about the forest. It was the month of Vaisakha (April/May) and the great sage Kauṇḍinya was just returning home after taking bath in the Ganges. At that time by Providence, Dhṛṣṭabuddhi, who was very aggrieved by distress and lamentation, happened to touch a drop of water falling from the sage's cloth. Dhṛṣṭabuddhi was immediately relieved of his sinful reactions. With folded hands and great humility he said to sage Kauṇḍinya, 'O great *brāhmaṇa,* I am the most sinful person. There is no sin that I have not committed. Now please instruct me about a topmost type of atonement which a most wretched person like me can easily perform. As a result of committing unlimited sinful activities till now I have been bereft of my house, wealth, relatives and friends. I am drowning in the ocean of mental agony.'

"After hearing these statements of Dhṛṣṭabuddhi the great sage Kauṇḍinya, feeling distress by seeing another's distress, said, 'I am telling you a sublime method by which all your sinful reactions can easily be nullified in a very short time; please hear me attentively. Mohinī Ekādaśī which occurs during the waxing moon in the month of April/May, totally destroys a mountain of sinful reactions as big as Mt. Sumeru accumulated from many many lifetimes. Therefore you should faithfully observe this Ekādaśī.'

"Hearing these words from the great sage, Dhṛṣṭabuddhi became joyful and properly observed that Ekādaśī according to the rules and regulations instructed by the sage. O best of kings! By observing this Mohinī Ekādaśī the most sinful Dhṛṣṭabuddhi soon became devoid of all sinful reactions, and after assuming a divine body he returned to the all-auspicious abode of Lord Viṣṇu by riding on the back of Garuḍa. O Rāmacandra! This vow certainly removes all kinds of illusion and the darkness of ignorance. Any piety accumulated by taking bath in the holy waters, giving in charity and performance of sacrifice cannot be compared with the piety one attains by observing this Mohinī Ekādaśī."

Chapter 13

Aparā Ekādaśī

The topics of Aparā Ekādaśī, which occurs during the waning moon in the month of May/June, are described in the *Brahmāṇḍa Purāṇa* in the conversation between Lord Kṛṣṇa and Mahārāja Yudhiṣṭhira.

Once Mahārāja Yudhiṣṭhira asked of Lord Kṛṣṇa, "O Lord Kṛṣṇa, O Janārdana, what is the name of the Ekādaśī that occurs during the waning moon in the month of May/June and what are its glories? Please describe all this to Me."

Lord Kṛṣṇa replied, "O Mahārāja Yudhiṣṭhira, you have asked Me an intelligent question that is actually beneficial for everyone. The name of this Ekādaśī is Aparā. O King! This Ekādaśī awards a tremendous amount of piety to those who observe it and destroys all their sinful reactions. By observing this Aparā Ekādaśī many grave sinful activities are destroyed such as killing a *brāhmaṇa*, killing a cow, killing an embryo through abortion, criticizing others, illicit sex life, speaking lies, giving false witness, bragging to others, reciting or teaching the *Vedas* for the sake of money, and concocting one's own scripture. A cheater, a pseudo astrologer, and a cheating physician are also as sinful as those who give false witness. All these sinful activities are totally eradicated by observing this Aparā Ekādaśī. Any *kṣatriya* who gives up his profession and runs away from the battlefield certainly falls down from his occupational duties and goes to hell. If such a person observes this Ekādaśī with faith he also attains the heavenly planet.

Lord Kṛṣṇa continued, "O King! A disciple who after receiving knowledge from his spiritual master engages in blaspheming his spiritual master certainly accumulates great sins. Such a condemned sinful person can be relieved from his sinful reactions by following the Aparā Ekādaśī and can attain the supreme destination. O King of Kings! The result one obtains by taking bath three times at Pushkar in the month of Kārtika, the piety one accumulates by taking bath at Prayāga in the month of January when the sun enters Capricorn, the results one obtains by observing the vow of Śivaratri at Kāśī and by offering oblations at the lotus feet of Viṣṇu at Gayā, and the auspicious results one obtains by taking bath in the river Gautami when the planet Jupiter enters Leo, by visiting Kedarnātha during Kumbha-mela, by visiting and worshiping Badrinātha, by taking bath at Kurukṣetra during a solar eclipse, and by giving elephants, horses, cows, gold and land in charity are all obtained easily by observing the vow of Aparā Ekādaśī. It is like the sharp axe for cutting down the tree of sinful activities and like a blazing forest fire for burning the fuel of sinful activities to ashes. It is like the brilliant sun for dissipating the darkness born of sinful activities and like the lion to a deer in the forest of sinful activities. O King! By observing this Aparā Ekādaśī and worshiping Lord Viṣṇu in His form as Trivikram, a person attains the all-auspicious abode of Lord Viṣṇu. Anyone who hears or reads the glories of this Ekādaśī, that I have described to you for the benefit of everyone, is relieved of all his sinful reactions."

Chapter 14

Nirjalā Ekādaśī

The description of Nirjalā Ekādaśī, which occurs during the month of May/June, is found in the *Brahma-vaivarta Purāṇa* in the conversation between Vyāsadeva and Bhīmasena.

Once Bhīmasena, the younger brother of Yudhiṣṭhira, inquired from the great sage Śrīla Vyāsadeva, "O most learned and worshipable grandfather, please hear my request. My elder brother Yudhiṣṭhira, mother Kuntidevi, brothers Arjuna, Nakula, and Sahadeva, and Draupadi do not eat anything on the day of Ekādaśī. They, especially Yudhiṣṭhira, always tell me that I should also fast on Ekādaśī. But I always tell them that though I know that to fast on Ekādaśī is an injunction of the scriptures, I cannot bear my hunger and therefore I am unable to fast. I can give in charity as per my capacity, I can worship Lord Keśava with proper rules and regulations, but I cannot fast. So please instruct me how can I obtain the result of Ekādaśī without having to fast."

On hearing these words of Bhīmasena, Śrī Vyāsadeva said, "O Bhīma! If you want to go to the heavenly planets and avoid the hellish planets, then you must refrain from eating on both the Ekādaśīs of each month."

Bhīma said, "O great sage! It is impossible for me to observe fast on 24 Ekādaśīs every year, as instructed by the Lord. What to speak of fasting day and night I cannot even tolerate my hunger for even a moment. The fire of hunger known as 'brika' is always present within my stomach, and it is extinguished only by voracious eating. But with great endeavor I can fast only one day in a year. Therefore please instruct me about a vow that I can follow to attain auspiciousness both in this life and the next."

Śrī Vyāsadeva said, "O King! You have already heard from me about the Vedic religious principles and the duties of the human beings. But in this age of Kali not everyone is capable of following those rules and regulations. Therefore I will tell you about a sublime method by which you can achieve great results. This method is the essence of all the *Purāṇas*. Anyone who observes the Ekādaśīs of waning and waxing moons by fasting never goes to hell."

Hearing Vyāsadeva's words, that strongest warrior Bhīmasena became frightened and shivered like a leaf on a banyan tree and said, "O grandfather! What should I do ? I am totally unable to fast twice a month throughout the year. Therefore, O my Lord, kindly instruct me about one vow that awards the most merit and how by observing it I can achieve all benefits."

Then Śrī Vyāsadeva replied, "The Ekādaśī which occurs during the waxing moon in the month of May/June during the sun's presence in either Taurus or Gemini Rasi is called Nirjalā Ekādaśī. One should observe total fast even from drinking water in this Ekādaśī. On this day one should perform *acamana* for purification by drinking that amount of water in which a single mustard seed or a drop of gold can be immersed. One should place the said amount of water in his palm held in such a way as to resemble a cow's ear. If one drinks more or less water than this, it will amount to drinking of wine.

"One must not eat anything at all on this Ekādaśī, otherwise his vow will be broken. One should not drink even water from the movement of sunrise from the day of Ekādaśī until the sunrise on the day of Dvādaśī. In this way if one strictly observes this Ekādaśī without drinking water then he can attain the results of observing all the Ekādaśīs of the year.

"In the early morning on the day of Dvādaśī one should take bath and give gold and water in charity to the *brāhmaṇas*. Thereafter the follower should gladly eat with the *brāhmaṇas*.

"O Bhimsena! Now please hear the about the piety one accumulates by observing this Ekādaśī. By following this Ekādaśī one can achieve the result of following all the Ekādaśīs throughout the year. Once Lord Viṣṇu, who holds a conch, a disc, a club and a lotus flower in His hand, told me, 'If a person gives up all varieties of religion and surrenders unto Me and follows this Nirjalā Ekādaśī which is very dear to Me, he is certainly relieved of all sinful reactions. One cannot attain the supreme destination by giving wealth in charity or attain any benefit by following *smarta* rules and regulations in the Kali-yuga. In fact the Vedic religious principles have been extinct in this age of Kali, which is polluted with various faults.'

"O son of Vayu! What more can I tell you? Eating is actually prohibited on all the Ekādaśīs, and even the drinking of water is prohibited on Nirjalā Ekādaśī. By observing this Ekādaśī one achieves the piety of visiting all the holy places. At the time of death such a person is not approached by the fierce-looking Yamadūtas, rather he is approached by the divine looking Viṣṇudutas to be transferred to the abode of Viṣṇu. If one gives water and cows in charity after observing this Ekādaśī then he is freed from all his sinful activities."

When the other Pāṇḍavas heard about the glories of this Ekādaśī they resolved to observe it. From that day onward Bhīmasena began observing this Nirjalā Ekādaśī, which became famous as Pāṇḍava Nirjalā, or Bhimseni Ekādaśī. By following this Ekādaśī sinful activities as huge as Sumeru or Mandra Mountain are at once burnt to ashes. O King! Lord Kṛṣṇa has declared that any pious activities such as taking bath in holy places, giving charity, chanting Vedic mantras, and performing sacrifices that are carried out on this Nirjalā Ekādaśī day become inexhaustible.

One who reads or hears the glories of this Ekādaśī with devotion goes back to the abode of Vaikuṇṭha. The result one attains by observing the vow of Amāvasyā conjoined with Pratipada and offering oblations to the forefathers during the solar eclipse is attained simply by hearing the glories of this Ekādaśī.

Chapter 15

Yoginī Ekādaśī

The glories of Yoginī Ekādaśī, which occurs during the waning moon in the month of June/July, are described in the *Brahma-vaivarta Purāṇa* in the conversation between Lord Kṛṣṇa and Mahārāja Yudhiṣṭhira.

Once Mahārāja Yudhiṣṭhira said, "O Supreme Lord! O Madhusūdana! I have heard the glories of Nirjalā Ekādaśī. Now I wish to hear about the Ekādaśī that occurs during the waning moon in the month of June/July."

Lord Kṛṣṇa replied, "O King! I will explain about the Ekādaśī that comes during the month of June/July. The name of this Ekādaśī is Yoginī and it destroys all one's grave sinful reactions and delivers one from the ocean of material existence.

"O best of kings! Now I will narrate a story from the *Purāṇa* to illustrate this truth. Kuvera, the King of Alakapuri, was a staunch devotee of Lord Śiva and regularly worshiped him. He had a Yakṣa gardener named Hema, whose wife was Visalakshi. Visalakshi was exquisitely beautiful, and Hema was very attached to her. Hema regularly gathered flowers from Manasa-sarovara Lake and gave them to Kuvera, the King of Yakṣas, for his worship of Lord Śiva. One day he brought flowers from Manasa-sarovara Lake and instead of giving them to Kuvera he remained at home, bound by the love of his dear wife.

"O King! As a result of this, Kuvera did not receive any flowers on that day. Meanwhile, the King of the Yakṣas, Kuvera waited six hours for Hema. Due to the absence of flowers, he could not complete the worship of Lord Śiva. Being extremely angry, the King immediately sent his messenger to find out the cause of the gardener's delay.

"After some time the Yakṣa messenger returned and said to the King. 'O master, Hema is enjoying the association of his wife at home.' On hearing these words Kuvera became very angry and immediately ordered his servants to bring Hema before him. On realizing that he has made a great mistake, Hema Mali became ashamed and with great fear he came before Kuvera and offered his respectful obeisances. Kuvera, whose entire body trembled and whose eyes became red with anger, said, 'O sinful one! O destroyer of religious principles, you have disregarded my most worshipable Lord Śrī Śankara and engaged in your own sense gratification, hence I am cursing you. You will be afflicted with white leprosy and you will remain separated from your dearmost wife forever. O low-class fool! You should immediately leave this place!'

"Being cursed by Kuvera, Hema Mali immediately fell from Alokapuri and took birth in this world. He became afflicted with white leprosy and suffered extremely miserable conditions. In such a condition and with intense mental agony and lack of food and water he went to a formidable dense forest. In that forest he suffered the pangs of hunger and thirst day and night. During the day he did not find any happiness and at night he could not sleep. He suffered great miseries both in winter and summer. But because he had helped worship Lord Śiva faithfully his memory remained in tact. Although he was engaged in various sinful activities he remembered his previous activities and his consciousness remained pure and alert.

"After wandering throughout the forest in this way he fortunately came to the Himalayan Mountain. While moving here and there, by Providence he had the good fortune of meeting the great sage Mārkaṇḍeya who is the best of the ascetics and whose duration of life is seven kalpas. Hema Mali, feeling very sinful, stood at a distance from the sage and repeatedly offered his humble obeisances. The kind-hearted sage Mārkaṇḍeya called that leprosy-ridden man before him and asked, 'O you! How did you get this dreadful affliction? What kind of sinful and condemned activities have you performed that you had to suffer such a miserable condition?'

"On hearing this, Hema Mali replied, 'O great sage! I am the gardener of Kuvera, the King of the Yakṣas. My name is Hema Mali. I use to collect flowers regularly from Manasa Sarovara Lake and give it to my master Kuvera. With these flowers Kuvera performed his worship of Lord Śiva. One day I was late to give flowers to my master because of remaining engaged in fulfilling my lusty desires with my wife. Therefore Kuvera, the King of the Yakṣas, became angry and cursed me. As a result of that curse I am profusely suffering the miseries of white leprosy and I have been separated from my wife. But now I do not know why this unfortunate soul has suddenly become fortunate enough to meet a great personality like you. I have heard that the hearts of the saintly persons are always afflicted by seeing the distress of others and they are always engaged in welfare activities. O great sage! With the desire to obtain auspicious results today this fallen soul has surrendered unto you. Please be kind and deliver him.'

"The great sage Mārkaṇḍeya spoke to him with compassion. 'O gardener! I am instructing you about a most auspicious and beneficial vow. You should observe the vow of Ekādaśī known as Yoginī that occurs during the waning moon in the month of June/July and by the influence of its piety you will certainly be liberated from the curse of suffering from leprosy. On hearing this instruction of the great sage Mārkaṇḍeya, Hema Mali became joyful and with feelings of gratitude he offered his humble obeisances to him. Thereafter he duly observed this sacred vow of Ekādaśī as the sage had instructed him. By the influence of this vow he regained his divine form. Then he returned home and reunited with his wife."

The result one obtains by feeding 88 thousand *brāhmaṇas* is attained by observing this Yoginī Ekādaśī. This Ekādaśī destroys all one's sinful reactions and awards one great piety.

Chapter 16

Śayanā Ekādaśī

The topics of Śayanā, Devasayani, or Padma, Ekādaśī are described in the *Bhaviṣyottara Purāṇa* in the conversation between Lord Kṛṣṇa and Mahārāja Yudhiṣṭhira.

Once Mahārāja Yudhiṣṭhira said, "O Keśava! What is the name of the Ekādaśī that occurs during the waxing moon in the month of June/July? Who is the worshipable deity for this sacred day, and what are the rules and regulations for observing this Ekādaśī? Please explain these details to me."

Lord Kṛṣṇa replied, "O maintainer of this world! This question was once asked by Śrī Nārada Muni to Lord Brahmā. Now please hear from Me the wonderful history which Lord Brahmā narrated to Nārada Muni in his reply.

"Once the great orator and best of the sages Nārada said to Lord Brahmā, 'O Father! What is the name of the Ekādaśī that occurs during the waxing moon in the month of June/July? Kindly explain how should I observe this Ekādaśī in order to please the Supreme Lord Viṣṇu.'

"Lord Brahmā replied, 'There is no other vow in this material world which is as sacred as the vow of Ekādaśī. It is extremely necessary for one to observe the vow of Ekādaśī in order to nullify all his sinful reactions. A person who does not observe Ekādaśī in this world certainly goes to hell. The Ekādaśī that occurs during the waxing moon in the month of June/July is called Devasayani, or Padma Ekādaśī. In order to please the Supreme Lord Hṛṣīkeśa one should follow this Ekādaśī.'

"It is stated in the *Purāṇa* there was a saintly emperor named Mandata who ruled the entire world. He was born in the dynasty of the sun-god, was extremely powerful and always stood up for the truth. This King maintained his subjects piously and affectionately as if they were his own children. In this pious king's kingdom there was no famine, drought or any kind of disease. All his subjects lived peacefully without any anxiety, and they were very prosperous. There was no wealth in the treasury of the King which was unlawfully earned. In this way the King and his subjects happily spent their days.

"After many years, due to Providence and some sinful activities, there was no rainfall in his kingdom for three consecutive years. As a result, people became afflicted with hunger due to lack of food and became full of anxiety. As a result of suffering from lack of food the performance of various sacrifices and the study of the *Vedas* came to a standstill. Then all the subjects came before the King and appealed, 'O King! Please hear our words which will ultimately benefit us. The water is addressed in the scriptures as 'Nara'. The Supreme Lord resides in 'ayana'. Therefore another name of the Supreme Lord is Nārāyaṇa. The Supreme Lord Viṣṇu is all-pervading in His form as clouds. He alone causes the rain fall. The food grains are produced from rain and the living entities subsist on grains. At present due to lack of these food grains your subjects are suffering and decreasing. O best of kings! Please find some remedy for our miserable condition and restore peace and prosperity among us.'

"The King replied, 'Whatever you have said is true. The food grains are considered like Brahman. Everything is sustained by food grains. The living entities of the entire world subsist on food grains. It is clearly stated in the *Purāṇas* and other scriptures that due to the sinful activities committed by the King he and his subjects suffer. Although I cannot ascertain my fault through my own consideration and intelligence, I will nevertheless try my best for the benefit of my subjects.'

"After speaking in this way King Mandata gathered some of his principle armies, and after offering obeisances to Brahmā, he entered the forest. Within the forest he regularly visited the *āśramas* of great sages and ascetics. While wandering in the forest in this way, one day by Providence the King met the great sage Aṅgirā, the son of Brahmā. Sage Aṅgirā was as effulgent as Brahmā and all the four directions were illuminated by his effulgence. As soon as the self-controlled king saw him, he immediately got down from his carrier and offered his respectful obeisances at the feet of the sage. Then the King folded his hands and offered prayers. The sage reciprocated by blessing the King.

"Thereafter the sage inquired from the King about the cause of his arrival and the well-being of his kingdom. The King replied, 'O Lord! I have been ruling my kingdom according to religious principles, but there has been no rainfall in my kingdom for the last three years. As a result my subjects are suffering from various miseries, and I have not been able to ascertain its cause in order to remove this cause. Today I have come to your lotus feet. Kindly tell me how my subjects can live peacefully and thus attain auspiciousness.'

"The sage Aṅgirā replied, 'O King! This present age of Satya-yuga is the best of all the *yugas*. In this *yuga* people worship the supreme Brahman. The fourfold religious principles are manifest in this *yuga*. No one except the *brāhmaṇas* are supposed to perform austerities in this *yuga*. In spite of this standard a *śūdra* in your kingdom is undergoing austerity. As a result of this unlawful conduct, you are facing its consequences in the form of drought. Therefore you should try to kill him and bring peace and prosperity into your kingdom.'

"The King said, ' O great sage it will be impossible for me to kill an innocent person who is engaged in performing austerity. Therefore please instruct me about some easy solution.'

"Then the sage replied, 'O King if this is the case, then observe the sacred Ekādaśī known as Padma, or Devasayani, which occurs during the waxing moon in the month of June/July. By the influence of this vow there will certainly be rainfall in your kingdom. This Ekādaśī awards one all-auspiciousness and perfection. It destroys all obstacles on the path to perfection. O King! You, along with your subjects, should observe this Ekādaśī.'

"After hearing these assuring words of the great sage, the King offered his obeisances and returned to his palace. Thereafter, in the month of Asadha or June/July, the King along his family members and subjects, properly observed this auspicious Padma, or Śayanā Ekādaśī. By the influence of this observance the rain poured down all over his kingdom. There was no more scarcity of water, and soon the entire world became filled with food grains, and by the mercy of the Supreme Lord Hṛṣīkeśa everyone lived happily. Therefore it is the duty of everyone to observe this sacred Ekādaśī, which awards everyone happiness and liberation. By hearing and reading the glories of this Ekādaśī all one's sinful reactions are destroyed.

"This Ekādaśī is also known as Viṣṇu Sayani Ekādaśī. In order to please Lord Viṣṇu the devotees observe this Ekādaśī with special devotion. They do not endeavor for material enjoyments or liberation rather they pray for pure devotional service to the Lord. The famous vow of Caturmasya begins from this Ekādaśī. The devotees observe the vow of Caturmasya by hearing and chanting the topics of the Lord for four months beginning from the day when Lord Hari goes to bed up to the day He wakes up."

Mahārāja Yudhiṣṭhira said to Lord Kṛṣṇa, "O Kṛṣṇa! Please tell me how one should observe this Śrī Viṣṇu Śayanā Vrata or Caturmasya-vrata."

Lord Kṛṣṇa replied, "O King! When the sun remains in the sign of Cancer, then Śrī Madhusūdana, the Lord of the entire universe, goes to bed, and when the sun goes to the sign of Libra, the Lord wakes up. The vow of Caturmasya commences from the day of Śayanā Ekādaśī. O King Yudhiṣṭhira! After taking bath one should dress Lord Viṣṇu in yellow garments. Then he should make a bed and cover it with white sheets to put the Lord to rest. First one should bath the Lord with five ingredients such as yogurt, milk, ghee, honey, and sugar water by the qualified *brāhmaṇas*. Then one should wipe the Lord's body with a cloth and apply fragrant sandalwood paste. Then he should worship the Lord by offering incense, a ghee lamp, and flowers with devotion.

'One can also begin observing the vow of Caturmasya either from the day of Ekādaśī, Dvādaśī, Pūrṇimā, Aṣṭamī, or Sankranti (when the sun enters into the sign of Cancer). The vow of Caturmasya ends on the day of Dvādaśī which falls the day after Utthāna Ekādaśī in the month of Kārtika. A person who observes the vow of Caturmasya while remembering Lord Hari goes back to the abode of Lord Viṣṇu sitting on an airplane as effulgent as the sun. Anyone who cleans the temple and the courtyard of the Lord, decorates them with flowers and creepers, and feeds the *brāhmaṇas* according to his capacity, at the end of the vow obtains inexhaustible happiness for seven life-times. By offering ghee lamps to the Lord during this vow, one can become fortunate and prosperous. One who chants Gayatri mantra one hundred and eight times in the temple of the Lord in three different times-morning, noon and evening no longer has to indulge in sinful activities. Lord Vyāsadeva becomes pleased with such a person and the practitioner returns to the abode of Viṣṇu. Anyone who donates twenty-eight or one hundred and eight pots of sesame seeds to the intelligent *brāhmaṇas* at the end of the vow becomes freed from his sinful reactions accumulated by his body, mind and speech. He becomes freed from all diseases and obtains intelligent children.

"A practitioner of devotional service should not sleep on a bedstead for the four months during which Lord Janārdana takes rest. It is prohibited to have sex during Caturmasya, except for the days of menstruation. One should observe this vow by fasting, eating only supper, eating only once a day or eating that which comes without asking for it. One who chants and sings before Lord Viṣṇu during Caturmasya goes to the planet of the Gandharvas. A person who gives up eating gur or juggery is blessed with sons and grandsons. By giving up oil, one becomes beautiful and his enemies are destroyed. By giving up the taste of bitter, pungent, sour, sweet, and salty preparations, one's ugliness and bodily odor is vanquished. Those who give up the enjoyment of flowers go to the heavenly planets and become Vidyadharas. By giving up the chewing of betel nuts one immediately becomes diseaseless. If one eats off the bare floor he attains the heavenly abode of Indra. If one gives up milk and yogurt for the pleasure of Kṛṣṇa, he goes to the supreme abode of Goloka. One who does not cut his nails or shave his head attains the good fortune of touching the lotus feet of Lord Viṣṇu. One who circumambulates the temple of the Lord returns to the abode of the Lord riding on a airplane carried by swans."

Chapter 17

Kāmikā Ekādaśī

The topics of Kāmikā Ekādaśī are described in the *Brahma-vaivarta Purāṇa* in the conversation between Lord Kṛṣṇa and Mahārāja Yudhiṣṭhira.

Mahārāja Yudhiṣṭhira said, "O Supreme Lord Kṛṣṇa! I have heard from You the glories of Devasayani Ekādaśī. Now I would like to hear about the Ekādaśī that occurs during the waning moon in the month of July/August. O Lord, kindly explain its glories."

Lord Kṛṣṇa replied, "O King! Please attentively hear the description of this sacred vow of Ekādaśī which removes all sins. In an ancient time Nārada Muni once asked Lord Brahmā about this same topic and inquired about the deity which is to be worshiped on that day and the process one must follow to observe this Ekādaśī."

Lord Brahmā, the spiritual master of the entire universe, replied, 'The Ekādaśī which occurs during the waning moon in the month of July/August is called Kāmikā Ekādaśī. By hearing the glories of this Ekādaśī one obtains the result of performing a Bajapeya sacrifice. On this auspicious day one should worship Lord Viṣṇu who holds a conch, a disc, a club and a lotus in His hands. The result one obtains by residing and bathing in holy places like near the Ganges, or in Kashi, Naimisaranya and Pushkar is obtained simply by worshiping Lord Viṣṇu on that day. The result not even obtainable by taking bath in Kedarnātha, Kurukṣetra or during the solar eclipse is easily obtained by worshiping Lord Kṛṣṇa on this day. Therefore it is the duty of everyone to strictly observe this Kāmikā Ekādaśī by worshiping Lord Viṣṇu.'

Just as the water cannot touch the lotus leaf, similarly, by the influence of this Kāmikā Ekādaśī a person can remain aloof from sins. Anyone who worships Lord Hari with Tulasi leaves is freed from all sins. Only by seeing Tulasi one's sinful reaction are destroyed, by touching Tulasi one's body become purified, by offering prayers to Tulasi one's diseases become cured, by bathing Tulasi one does not have to fear from Yamarāja, the Lord of death, by planting Tulasi one becomes fortunate enough to reside with Lord Kṛṣṇa and by offering Tulasi leaves at the feet of the Supreme Lord one attains pure devotional service. Even Chitra Gupta is unable to estimate the piety of one who offers obeisances and a ghee lamp to such a Tulasi on the day of Ekādaśī. The sin of killing a *brāhmaṇa* or an embryo is destroyed as a secondary result of observing this Kāmikā Ekādaśī. One who hears or reads the glories of this Ekādaśī with faith certainly attains the abode of Viṣṇu.

Chapter 18

Pavitrā Ekādaśī

The glories of Pavitrā Ekādaśī are described in the *Bhaviṣyottara Purāṇa* in the conversation between Lord Kṛṣṇa and Mahārāja Yudhiṣṭhira.

Once Mahārāja Yudhiṣṭhira asked Kṛṣṇa, "O Madhusūdana, the killer of the Madhu demon, what is the name and the glories of the Ekādaśī that occurs during the waxing moon in the month of July/August? Please explain this to me in detail."

Lord Kṛṣṇa replied, "O King! The name of this sacred Ekādaśī is Pavitrā Ekādaśī. Now please hear attentively about the topics of this Ekādaśī, which destroys one's sinful reactions. By hearing the glories of this Ekādaśī, one obtains the result of performing a Vajapeya sacrifice.

"Long ago in the beginning of Dvāpara-yuga there was a King named Mahījit who ruled the kingdom named Māhiṣmatīpuri. The king had no sons and was unhappy while conducting his activities. A married man who has no son has no happiness either in this life or in the next. For many years the King tried to get a son, but he was not fortunate enough to get a jewel-like son who would give him all pleasure.

"One day, realizing his own pathetic condition, the King called his subjects whom he treated as his children to the royal assembly and said to them,' O dear subjects, I have never committed any sinful activity in my life, I did not increase my treasury by unlawfully earned wealth, I did not plunder the wealth of the *brāhmaṇas* and the demigods, rather I have conquered this world by following the proper code of conduct, and I have maintained all of you like my own children, I have never hesitated to award due punishment even to my dear ones like my brother and relatives according to their faults, and I have shown due respect even to my enemy if he was gentle and pious. O *brāhmaṇas,* in spite of traveling on the religious path like this, I am bereft of a son. Please consider carefully the reason behind this and advise me.'

"After hearing these lamenting words of King Mahījit, the King's *brāhmaṇa* advisers discussed the subject matter among themselves and decided that for the benefit of the King they would go to the forest and visit the *āśramas* of the great sages who know the past, present and future. After entering the forest and wandering here and there, they came across various *āśramas* of great sages. Finally they met Lomaśa Muni, who was engaged in severe austerities. His body was spiritual and full of bliss, and he strictly observed the vow of fasting. He was self-controlled and knew the science of eternal religious principles, and he was well conversant with the knowledge of the scriptures. His duration of life was as long as that of Brahmā, and he was an effulgent saint. When a kalpa of Brahmā passes, one hair (*loma*) falls from his body. That is why the name of the sage is Lomaśa. The sage Lomaśa was the knower of past, present, and future.

"Enchanted by this great sage, the advisors of the King offered their obeisances to him and spoke with humility. 'O great sage! Due to our great fortune we have met a great soul like you.' The sage Lomaśa inquired, 'Who are you all? Why have you come here? Why are you praising me like this?' The *brāhmaṇas* replied, 'O great sage! We have come to you to solve our dilemma. O Lord! Our king, Mahījit, has no sons. We are his subjects, and we are treated by the King as his own children. We are feeling disturbed on seeing the distress of the King. O best of the *brāhmaṇas,* we want to strictly undergo austerity here. It is the good fortune of the King that today we have met a great personality like you. By the *darśana* of a great personality, a man certainly attains all perfections. Please instruct us in such a way that our sonless king can have a son.'

"After hearing their sincere prayers, the sage Lomaśa entered into a deep meditation for a movement and immediately understood the King Mahījit's previous life. He then said that in his previous life this king was a poor *vaiśya,* or merchant. He committed a sinful deed. Once while traveling from village to village in the course of his business he became overwhelmed with thirst. It was the midday of Dvādaśī in the month of July. Soon he found a beautiful lake and decided to drink its water. At that time a cow and her newly born calf came there to drink water. As the cow began to drink water from the lake the merchant immediately drove her away and began to drink water himself. As a result of obstructing the thirsty cow from drinking water, the merchant had committed a sin. For this reason, though the merchant has now been born as King Mahījit, by the influence of his piety he cannot get a son.

"On hearing these words of the great sage, the King's advisors said, 'O great sage! It is stated in the *Purāṇas* that by the influence of piety all one's sinful reactions are counteracted. Therefore please instruct us in such a way that all the sinful reactions of the King will be destroyed and he can obtain a son.'

"The great sage Lomaśa replied, 'There is a famous auspicious Ekādaśī known as Pavitrā Ekādaśī which occurs during the waxing moon in the month of July/August. You and your King should properly observe this Ekādaśī. Thereafter you should give the piety that you earn by observing this Ekādaśī to your King. If you follow my instruction, then the King will certainly be blessed with a son. After hearing these words from sage Lomaśa, all the King's advisors became happy and satisfied. They offered their obeisances to the sage and returned home. Then they met King Mahījit and explained to him in detail what they had heard from the great sage Lomaśa.

"Thereafter, when the proper time arrived, the King's advisors remembered the advice of the sage and properly observed the vow of Pavitrā Ekādaśī with the King. On the day of Dvādaśī they gave away their accumulated piety to the King as advised by the sage. By the influence of this piety the Queen became pregnant and in due course of time she gave birth to a beautiful son.

"O King Yudhiṣṭhira! Anyone who observes this sacred Ekādaśī is relieved from sinful reactions and becomes happy both in this life and in the next. One who hears the glories of this Ekādaśī obtains the happiness derived from having a son in this life and goes back to Godhead in his next life."

Chapter 19

Annadā Ekādaśī

The glories of Annadā Ekādaśī are described in the *Brahma-vaivarta Purāṇa* in the conversation between Lord Kṛṣṇa and Mahārāja Yudhiṣṭhira.

Mahārāja Yudhiṣṭhira said, "O Kṛṣṇa! What is the name of the Ekādaśī that occurs during the waning moon in the month of August/September? Please be kind to me and explain this."

Lord Kṛṣṇa replied, "O King! Hear me with full attention. The name of this auspicious Ekādaśī, which removes all one's sins, is Annadā Ekādaśī. One who observes the vow of this Ekādaśī and worships Lord Hṛṣīkeśa, the master of the senses, becomes free from the reactions of his sinful activities.

"In an ancient time there was a famous emperor named Hariścandra. He was very truthful and honest. Due to some unknown deeds and in order to protect the validity of his promise, he lost his great kingdom. He even had to sell himself, his wife, and his son. O King! This pious emperor became a menial servant of a dog-eater. Still he maintained his firm faith in truthfulness. By the order of his master, the dog-eater, he began to accept the cloths from the dead bodies in the crematorium as his salary. In spite of engaging in such a low-class service, he did not fall from his truthfulness and proper code of conduct. In this way he passed many years.

"Then one day the King began to contemplate with great unhappiness. 'What should I do? Where should I go? How will I be delivered?' Seeing the great distress of the King, the great sage Gautama came to him. On seeing the great sage, the King thought that Lord Brahmā has created the *brāhmaṇas* for the benefit of others. The King then offered his respectful obeisances to that best of the *brāhmaṇas* and stood before him with folded hands. Then he narrated his entire pitiful story to sage Gautama.

"The great sage Gautama was astonished to hear the pathetic story of the King and said, 'O King! The Annadā Ekādaśī, which occurs during the waning moon in the month of August/September, is extremely auspicious and removes all sins. It is your good fortune that this Ekādaśī is coming soon. You should observe this Ekādaśī by fasting and staying awake at night. As a result of this, all your sinful reaction will soon be eradicated. O best of kings! Only by your influence I have come here.'

"After instructing King Hariścandra in this way, the great sage Gautama disappeared. Thereafter, according to the instruction of the sage, the King observed the vow of Annadā Ekādaśī and became liberated from all his sinful reactions."

Lord Kṛṣṇa concluded, "O lion-like King! The wonderful influence of this Ekādaśī is such that one immediately exhausts the sufferings that he was destined to suffer for many, many years. By the influence of this Ekādaśī, King Hariścandra regained his wife and his dead son became alive. The demigods began to play drums and shower flowers from the sky. Thereafter, by the influence of this Ekādaśī, the King enjoyed his kingdom without any impediment. Eventually the King went to the spiritual world along with his relatives, associates, and subjects. O King! Anyone who observes this Ekādaśī will become free from all sins and will go to the spiritual world."

By hearing or reading the glories of this Ekādaśī, one can obtain the result of performing a horse sacrifice.

Chapter 20

Pārśva Ekādaśī

The glories of Pārśva Ekādaśī, which is also known as Parivartini Ekādaśī or Vāmana Ekādaśī, are described in *Brahma-vaivarta Purāṇa* in the conversation between Lord Kṛṣṇa and Mahārāja Yudhiṣṭhira.

Mahārāja Yudhiṣṭhira asked Lord Kṛṣṇa, "What is the name of the Ekādaśī that occurs during the waxing moon in the month of August/September? How one should observe this Ekādaśī, and what is the merit one obtains by observing it? Please explain to me all these in details."

Lord Kṛṣṇa replied, "O King! The Ekādaśī that occurs during the waxing moon in the month of August/September is called Pārśva Ekādaśī. This Ekādaśī is very auspicious. It awards one liberation and takes away all one's sins. Just by hearing the glories of this Ekādaśī, all the sinful reactions of a person are vanquished. The piety one obtains by observing this Ekādaśī cannot be obtained even by performing a Vajapeya sacrifice. This Ekādaśī is also known as Jayanti Ekādaśī. One who worships Lord Vāmana Deva with devotion on this day is worshiped by the inhabitants of the three worlds. A person who worships the lotus-eyed Lord Viṣṇu with a lotus flower undoubtedly goes back to the abode of the Lord. On this Ekādaśī the sleeping Lord turns from left side to right side. Therefore this Ekādaśī is known as Pārśva Parivartini ("changing sides") Ekādaśī."

Mahārāja Yudhiṣṭhira said, "O Janārdana! In spite of hearing Your description, I still have some doubts. O Lord of Lords! How do You sleep, and how do You change sides? What are the procedures for observing the vow of Caturmasya? What should people do when You are sleeping? Why did You bind Bali Mahārāja with ropes? O my Lord! Please describe all this to me in detail and remove my doubts."

Lord Kṛṣṇa replied, "O lion-like King! In Tretā-yuga there was a great devotee of Mine named Bali. Although born in a demoniac family, he regularly worshiped Me and offered Me various prayers. He also worshiped the *brāhmaṇas* and performed sacrifices. Soon he became so prominent that he defeated Indra, the King of heaven, and conquered the heavenly planet. Then Indra along with the other demigods and the sages approached Me. By their prayer I assumed the form of a dwarf (Vāmana) and went to the sacrificial arena of King Bali dressed as a small *bramacārī*.

"I asked Bali for three steps of land in charity. When Bali requested Me to ask for something more than simply three steps of land, I exhibited My determination to remain satisfied with what I had asked for. Without further consideration, King Bali and his wife, Vindhyawali, gave Me the three steps of land in charity. Due to being the Supreme Personality of Godhead, Lord Vāmanadeva gradually began to expand His body. With one step He covered the seven lower planetary systems, and with His second step He covered the entire planetary system including the entire sky. When Vāmanadeva asked for a place to set His third step, King Bali, with folded hands, offered his own head. Then Lord Vāmanadeva placed His third step on the head of King Bali. Being fully satisfied by his humility, I blessed him that I would constantly live with him.

"On the day of this Ekādaśī, which occurs during the waxing moon in the month of August/September, a deity form of Vāmanadeva was installed in the residence of King Bali. Another form of Mine has been established in the bed of Ananta Sesa in the ocean of milk. The Supreme Lord sleeps for four months beginning from Śayanā Ekādaśī up to Utthāna Ekādaśī. One should offer special worship to the Lord during these four months. One should properly observe each and every Ekādaśī."

By observing this Ekādaśī, one obtains the result of performing one thousand horse sacrifices.

Chapter 21

Indirā Ekādaśī

The glories of Indirā Ekādaśī are described in *Brahma-vaivarta Purāṇa* in the conversation between Lord Kṛṣṇa and Mahārāja Yudhiṣṭhira.

Mahārāja Yudhiṣṭhira said, "O Kṛṣṇa! O Madhusūdana! O Killer of the demon Madhu! What is the name of the Ekādaśī that occurs during the waning moon in the month of September/October? What are the rules and regulations for observing this Ekādaśī, and what is the merit one gains by observing it?"

Lord Kṛṣṇa replied, "The name of this sacred Ekādaśī is Indirā Ekādaśī. By observing this Ekādaśī one can deliver his degraded forefathers and all of his own sinful reactions are eradicated.

"O King! There was a king named Indrasena, who lived in Satya-yuga. He was very expert in subduing his enemies and ruled his kingdom, Māhiṣmatīpuri, with great prosperity. Surrounded by his children and grandchildren, he lived happily. He was always attached to the devotional service of Lord Viṣṇu. Being a devotee constantly absorbed in spiritual knowledge, the King spent his time chanting the holy names of Śrī Govinda, the bestower of liberation.

"One day as the King was happily sitting on his royal throne, Śrī Nārada Muni suddenly appeared before him from the sky. On seeing the great sage Nārada, the King immediately stood up with folded hands and then offered his respectful obeisances to him. The king then duly worshiped the sage by sixteen ingredients. After the sage was happily seated, he asked Indrasena, 'O great King! Is everyone happy and prosperous in your kingdom? Is your mind fixed in religious principles, and are you engaged in devotional service to Viṣṇu?'

"The King replied, 'O best of the sages! Everything is well and auspicious by your mercy. Today my life has become successful by your *darśana* and my performance of sacrifices has born fruit. O sage among the demigods! Please tell me the cause of your visit.'

"After hearing these humble words of the King, Nārada Muni said, 'O lion-like King! Now hear about an wonderful incident that had happened to me. O best of kings! Once I went to the abode of Yamarāja from the abode of Lord Brahmā. Yamarāja greeted me respectfully and worshiped me properly. After I was comfortably seated, I offered prayers to the pious truthful Yamarāja. Then I saw your greatly pious father in the assembly of Yamarāja. As a result of breaking a vow, your father had to go there. O King! He me a message and requested me to convey it to you. He said, 'Indrasena, the King of Māhiṣmatīpuri, is my son. O Lord, please tell him that due to some sinful activities committed in my previous life I am now living in the abode of Yamarāja. Therefore he should observe the vow of Indirā Ekādaśī and give away its piety to me. Then I will be released from my present condition of life.' Nārada Muni continued, 'O King! This is your father's request to you. In order to deliver your father to the spiritual world, you should observe the vow of Indirā Ekādaśī.'

"Then King Indrasena said, 'O sage among the demigods, kindly explain to me the procedure for following this Indirā Ekādaśī.'

"Nārada Muni replied, 'On the day before Ekādaśī one should take bath early in the morning and faithfully offer oblations to the forefathers for their satisfaction. On that day one should eat only once and sleep on the floor at night. On the day of Ekādaśī one should rise early in the morning, brush his teeth, wash his hands and mouth and take bath. Thereafter he should take a vow to not indulge in any kind of material enjoyment and thus observe a total fast. He should also pray to the Lord, saying, 'O lotus-eyed one, I take shelter of you.'

"Thereafter at noon, in front of *śālagrāma-śilā* he should offer oblations to his forefather according to proper rules and regulations. Then he should worship the *brāhmaṇas* by feeding them sumptuously and then giving them *dakṣīṇa*. At the end one should give the remnants of the oblations to the cows. During the day one should worship Lord Hṛṣīkeśa by offering sandalwood paste, flowers, incense, lamp, and foodstuffs with devotion. One should remain awake that night while chanting, hearing, and remembering the names, forms, qualities, and pastimes of the Supreme Lord. The next morning one should worship Lord Hari and feed the *brāhmaṇas*. Thereafter one should break his fast by eating along with his brothers, children, grandchildren, and relatives while maintaining silence. O King! If you follow this Ekādaśī as I have just described, then your father will certainly attain the abode of Viṣṇu.' After speaking in this way, Nārada Muni disappeared.

"According to the instructions of Nārada Muni, King Indrasena strictly observed this Ekādaśī accompanied by his children, servants, and others. As a result of observing this Ekādaśī, flowers showered from the sky and the father of King Indrasena immediately rode on the back of Garuḍa to the abode of Lord Viṣṇu. Then the saintly King Indrasena ruled his kingdom without any impediment, and at the end of his life he entrusted the kingdom to his son and personally returned to the spiritual world. Such are the glories of Indirā Ekādaśī. Anyone who reads or hears the glories of this Ekādaśī becomes free from all sinful reactions and ultimately returns to the abode of Viṣṇu."

Chapter 22

Pāśāṅkuśā Ekādaśī

The glories of Pāśāṅkuśā Ekādaśī, which occurs during the waxing moon in the month of September/October, are described in the *Brahma-vaivarta Purāṇa* in the conversation between Lord Kṛṣṇa and Mahārāja Yudhiṣṭhira.

Mahārāja Yudhiṣṭhira said, "O Madhusūdana, what is the name of the Ekādaśī that occurs during the waxing moon in the month of September/October? Please be kind and explain this to me."

Lord Kṛṣṇa replied, "O best of kings! The name of this Ekādaśī is Pāśāṅkuśā Ekādaśī. Now please hear the glories of this Ekādaśī that destroys all one's sins. Some people also call this Ekādaśī Papankusa Ekādaśī. One should particularly worship Lord Padmanabha on the day of this Ekādaśī. This Ekādaśī awards a person heavenly pleasures, liberation, and his desired results. Just by chanting the holy names of Lord Viṣṇu one can attain the piety of visiting all the holy places on the earth. If a conditioned soul, in spite of indulging in various sinful activities due to illusion, takes shelter and offers obeisances at the lotus feet of Lord Hari who is expert in delivering the fallen souls, then such a person does not have to go to hell.

"Those Vaiṣṇavas who criticize Lord Śiva and those Saivaites who criticize Lord Viṣṇu will both undoubtedly go to hell. The result one obtains by performing one thousand horse sacrifices or by performing one hundred Rājasūya sacrifices cannot be equal to one sixteenth portion of the piety one obtains by following this Ekādaśī. There is no piety in this world which is equal to the piety earned by observing this Ekādaśī. Therefore there is no other day as sanctified as this day of Ekādaśī, which is very dear to Lord Padmanabha.

"O King! As soon as a person fails to observe Ekādaśīs, sins begin to reside in his body. This Ekādaśī awards its follower heavenly pleasures, liberation, freedom from disease, beautiful women, wealth, and food grains. O maintainer of the earth! If one observes this Ekādaśī and remains awake on that night, he easily goes to the abode of Lord Viṣṇu."

Lord Kṛṣṇa continued, "O best of kings! By observing the vow of this Ekādaśī one can deliver ten generations from his mothers family, ten generations from his father's family, and ten generations from his wife's family. If a person observes this Ekādaśī either in his childhood, youth, or old age, he does not suffer the miseries of material existence. One who strictly observes this Pāśāṅkuśā, or Papankusa Ekādaśī, is relieved of all sinful reactions and at the end of life he returns to the abode of Lord Viṣṇu. If a person gives away gold, sesame seeds, land, cows, food grains, water, umbrellas, or shoes in charity, then such a person does not have to go to the abode of Yamarāja. Anyone who spends his day without engaging in pious activities is like a dead man although he is breathing. His breathing is compared to the bellows of the blacksmith.

"O best of kings! A person who digs wells and lakes for the benefit of others, who donates land and houses, and who performs other pious activities such as sacrifices is not subjected to the punishment of Yamarāja. It is a result of piety only that people live long lives, become rich, take birth in high-class families, and become free from disease. The purport is that the direct result of observing Ekādaśī is to attain devotional service to Kṛṣṇa, and the indirect result is to attain temporary material benefits."

Chapter 23

Ramā Ekādaśī

The glories of Ramā Ekādaśī are described in the *Brahma-vaivarta Purāṇa* in the conversation between Lord Kṛṣṇa and Mahārāja Yudhiṣṭhira.

Mahārāja Yudhiṣṭhira said, "O Janārdana! What is the name of the Ekādaśī that occurs during the waning moon in the month of October/November? Please explain this to me."

Lord Kṛṣṇa replied, "O lion among Kings! The name of this Ekādaśī is Ramā Ekādaśī and it vanquishes all one's sinful reactions. Now please hear the glories of this sacred Ekādaśī.

"Long, long ago there was a famous king named Mucukunda. He was a good friend of Indra, the King of heaven. He also had friendship with personalities like Yamarāja, Varuna, Kuvera and Vibhisana. This king was very truthful and always attached to the devotional service of Lord Viṣṇu. He ruled his kingdom with proper code of conduct.

"In due course of time, King Mucukunda begot a daughter. She was named after the best river, Candrabhaga. In due course of time, she was married to a handsome person named Shobhana, who was the son of Candrasena. One day Shobhana came to the house of his father-in-law on the day of the Ekādaśī. Candrabhaga became greatly worried and contemplated, 'O my Lord! What will happen now ? My husband is very weak and he cannot tolerate hunger. Moreover my father is also very strict. On the day before Ekādaśī my father usually sends his servant to announce that no one can eat on the day of Ekādaśī.'

"When Shobhana heard about this custom, he said to his dear wife, 'O dear one! What should I do now? What can I do so that my life is protected and the order of the King is not transgressed?'

Candrabhaga replied, 'O my lord! What to speak of the human beings, even the elephants, horses, and other animals in the kingdom of my father will not be allowed to eat anything today. O husband, how then can the human beings possibly eat? O respected husband! If you must eat today, then you will have to go back to your house. Therefore consider carefully and take a decision.'

"After hearing the words of his wife, Shobhana said, 'What you have said is indeed true, but I wish to observe this Ekādaśī. Whatever is destined for me will certainly happen.'

"Considering in this way, Shobhana decided to observe this sacred Ekādaśī, but he became overwhelmed with hunger and thirst. When the sun set, all the Vaiṣṇavas and pious human beings became very happy. O lion among Kings! They happily spent the entire night chanting and worshiping the Supreme Lord. But it was intolerable for Shobana to pass that night and thus he died just before sunrise. King Mucukunda completed Shobhana's funeral rites with royal prestige by burning him with fragrant sandalwood. According to the order of her father, Candrabhaga did not burn herself in the funeral fire, in other words, she did not die with her husband. After completing her husband's *śrāddha* ceremony, Candrabhaga continued to live at the house of her father.

"O King! Meanwhile, by the influence of observing Ramā Ekādaśī, Shobhana became the King of the beautiful city of Devapura, which was situated at the peak of Mandara mountain. He began to live in an opulent residence with pillars made of gold and bedecked with jewels and walls decorated with gems and crystals. A beautiful white umbrella was held over his head, which was decorated with a golden crown bedecked with jewels. His ears were decorated with earrings, his neck was decorated with a necklace, and his arms were decorated with golden armlets. Decorated in this way, Shobhana sat on the royal throne. He was always served by the Gandharvas and Apsarās and appeared just like Indra, the King of heaven.

"One day a *brāhmaṇa* named Somasharma, a resident of Mucukundapura, arrived in the kingdom of Shobhana in the course of traveling to the holy places. Considering Shobhana as the son-in-law of King Muchkunda, the *brāhmaṇa* approached him. As soon as the King saw him, he stood up with folded hands and then offered his respectful obeisances to the *brāhmaṇa*. Thereafter Shobhana inquired from the *brāhmaṇa* about his well-being and the well-being of his father-in-law, Mucukunda, his wife, Candrabhaga, and all the residents of Mucukundapur. He informed the King that everyone was living in peace and harmony. In great amazement, the *brāhmaṇa* said, ' King! I have never before seen such a beautiful city as this. Please tell me how you have obtained such a kingdom.'

"The King replied, 'By the influence of observing Ramā Ekādaśī, which occurs during the waning moon in the month of October/November, I have received this temporary kingdom. O best of the *brāhmaṇas,* please advise me how my kingdom can remain permanently. I think because I observed the Ekādaśī without faith hence I have received this unsteady kingdom. Please explain these topics to Candrabhaga, the beautiful daughter of King Mucukunda. I think she is capable of making it steady.'

"After hearing these words of King Shobhana, the *brāhmaṇa* returned to Mucukundapur and told everything to Candrabhaga in detail. When Candrabhaga heard the whole incident she became extremely joyful and said to the *brāhmaṇa*, 'O great *brāhmaṇa*! Your statements appear to be just like a dream!' Then the *brāhmaṇa* Somaśharma said, 'O daughter! I have personally seen your husband at Devpuri plus his entire kingdom which is as bright as the sun, but he told me that his kingdom was not steady. Therefore you should try to make his kingdom steady by any means.' Candrabhaga said, 'O respected *brāhmaṇa,* please take me there because I have developed an intense desire to see my husband. I will make his kingdom steady on the strength of my piety. O twice-born! Please make some arrangement so that I can meet him for by helping the separated to meet, one accumulates piety.

"Thereafter Somasharma took Candrabhaga to the *āśrama* of Vamadeva which was situated near Mandara Mountain. After hearing the whole story from the bright-faced Candrabhaga, Vamadeva initiated her with Vedic mantras. By the influence of the mantras received from sage Vamadeva and by the piety accumulated as a result of observing Ekādaśī, Candrabhaga obtained a spiritual body. Thereafter Candrabhaga happily went before her husband.

"Upon seeing his wife, Shobana became extremely pleased and satisfied. Candrabhaga said, 'O my respected husband, please hear my beneficial words. I have been strictly observing Ekādaśī from the age of eight at the house of my father. May that accumulated piety make your kingdom steady and let it continue to prosper until the time of annihilation. Thereafter having received a divine body decorated with opulent ornaments, she began to enjoy the association of her husband. By the influence of Ramā Ekādaśī, Shobana also received a divine body and began to enjoy with his wife at the peak of Mandara Mountain. Therefore, O King, this Ramā Ekādaśī is just like a wishfulfilling cow or a touch stone.'

Lord Kṛṣṇa continued, "O King, I have thus explained to you the glories of the auspicious Ramā Ekādaśī. A person who strictly observes the vow of this Ekādaśī is undoubtedly freed from the sin of killing a *brāhmaṇa*. Just as black cows and white cows both give white milk similarly Ekādaśīs of the waning moon and Ekādaśīs of the waxing moon both award liberation to the followers. Anyone who hears the glories of this Ekādaśī becomes liberated from all sinful reactions and happily resides in the abode of Lord Viṣṇu."

Chapter 24

Utthāna Ekādaśī

The glories of Utthāna, or Prabodhinī, Ekādaśī are described in the *Skanda Purāṇa* in the conversation between Lord Brahmā and Nārada Muni.

Once Lord Brahmā said to Nārada Muni, "O best of the sages! Please hear about the glories of Utthāna Ekādaśī which destroys all one's sinful reactions, increases one's piety and awards liberation. O best among the *brāhmaṇas*! The supremacy of the Ganges was intact as long as Utthāna Ekādaśī, which occurs during the waxing moon in the month of October/November and which burns all one's sins into ashes, did not manifest in this world. The influence of the ocean's and lake's piety was matchless as long as Utthāna Ekādaśī did not manifest. The result one obtains by performing one thousand horse sacrifices and one hundred Rājasūya sacrifices can easily be obtained by observing this Ekādaśī."

After hearing these words of Lord Brahmā, Nārada Muni said, "O dear father! Please tell me what the merit is for one who eats only once a day, or by taking supper in the evening or by completely fasting?"

Lord Brahmā replied, "If one eats only once a day then all the sinful reactions of his one lifetimes are destroyed. If one eats only supper then the sinful reactions of his two lifetime are destroyed, and by fasting completely one can destroy the sinful reactions of his seven lifetimes.

"O dear son! This Utthāna Ekādaśī awards everything that is unseen, undesired and rare within the three worlds. This Ekādaśī burns to ashes grave sins which are as big as Mandara Mountain. O lion among sages, if a person accumulates any piety on this day of Ekādaśī then he obtains results equal to Sumeru Hill. In the body of those who do not pray to the Lord, who are fallen from their vows, who are atheistic, who blaspheme the *Vedas*, who pollute the religious scriptures, who enjoy another's wife and who are foolish, the religious principles cannot remain. One should not indulge in sinful activities, rather he should engage in pious activities. If one is inclined towards pious activities, his religious principles are not destroyed. For one who confidently follows the vow of Utthāna Ekādaśī, the sinful reactions of his one hundred lifetimes are vanquished. If one remains awake on the night of Utthāna Ekādaśī then his past, present and future generations return to the abode of Viṣṇu.

"O Nārada! A person who does not observe the vow of Ekādaśī in the month of Kārtika and does not worship Lord Viṣṇu, has all his accumulated piety totally destroyed. O best of the *brāhmaṇas*! One should certainly worship Lord Viṣṇu in the month of Kārtika. If one eats foodstuff cooked by himself in the month of Kārtika, he obtains the result of Candrayana vrata. If one engages in hearing and chanting the topics of Lord Viṣṇu in the month of Kārtika attains the result of donating one hundred cows. By regularly studying the scriptures one achieves the result of performing one thousand sacrifices. A person who hears the topics of the Lord and then gives *dakṣīṇa* to the speaker according to his capacity goes to the eternal abode of the Lord.

Nārada Muni said, "O Lord! Kindly explain to me the procedure for observing Ekādaśī." Grandfather Brahmā replied, "O best of the twice-born, one should rise early in the morning during Brahma Muhurtha and after washing his mouth and taking bath he should worship Lord Keśava. Then he should take a vow while chanting a mantra as follows, ' I will fast on the day of Ekādaśī and I will only eat on the day of Dvādaśī. O Puṇḍarīkākṣa! O Acyuta! I surrender unto You. Please protect me.'

"One should gladly observe the vow of Ekādaśī with devotion and at night one should remain awake near Lord Viṣṇu. While remaining awake at night one should hear and chant the transcendental qualities of the Lord. One should give up all kinds of greediness on the day of Ekādaśī. Any pious person who follows these instructions attains the supreme destination.

Lord Brahmā continued, "If one worships Lord Janārdana with kadamba flowers, he does not go to the abode of Yamarāja. If one worships Lord Garuḍadvaja or Lord Viṣṇu with rose flowers in the month of Kārtika he certainly gets liberation. If one worships the Lord with bakula and ashoka flowers then he becomes freed from lamentation for as long as the sun and the moon rise in the sky. If one worships the Lord with sami leaves he escapes the punishment of Yamarāja. If one worships Lord Viṣṇu, Who is the controller of the demigods with *campaka* flowers during the rainy season then he will not have to take birth again within the material world. If one offers yellow colored ketaki flowers to Lord Viṣṇu then all his sinful reactions accumulated from millions of lifetimes are destroyed. If one offers red colored fragrant hundred-petaled lotus flowers to Lord Jagannātha then he returns to the abode of the Lord known as Svetadvipa.

"O best of the *brāhmaṇas*! One should remain awake on the night of Ekādaśī. On the day of Dvādaśī one should worship Lord Viṣṇu and complete his vow by feeding the *brāhmaṇas*."

According to one's ability if one worships his spiritual master and gives him charity then the Supreme Lord becomes pleased with him.

Chapter 25

Padminī Ekādaśī

Mahārāja Yudhiṣṭhira said, "O Kṛṣṇa! O Janārdana! Please describe to me what the name is of the Ekādaśī that occurs during the waning moon of the extra leap year month. What is the procedure for observing this Ekādaśī and what merit does one gain by observing it?"

Lord Kṛṣṇa replied, "O King! The name of this sacred Ekādaśī is Padminī Ekādaśī. If one strictly observes this Ekādaśī he returns to the abode of Lord Padmanabha. This Ekādaśī counteracts all one's sinful reactions. Even Lord Brahmā is unable to describe all the results of this Ekādaśī.

"However, long, long ago, Lord Brahmā described the glories of Padminī Ekādaśī, which awards its followers opulence and liberation, to the great sage Nārada."

Lord Kṛṣṇa continued, "One should begin to observe this vow on the day of Daśamī or the day before Ekādaśī. One should not eat foodstuff cooked by others, he should not eat in a plate made of bell metal, and he should not eat urad dal, chickpeas, spinach and honey on the day before Ekādaśī. One should eat boiled sunned rice with ghee and rock salt. One should sleep on the floor and observe strict celibacy on the day of Ekādaśī.

"On the day of Ekādaśī one should rise early in the morning, brush his teeth and take bath. Thereafter he should worship the Supreme Lord with sandalwood paste, incense, a lamp, aguru, camphor and water and one should chant the holy names and glories of the Lord. One should not indulge in useless talks. If one drinks water or milk on the day of the Ekādaśī which occurs during the extra leap year month then his vow is spoiled. One should remain awake at night on Ekādaśī and glorify the holy names and qualities of the Supreme Lord. By remaining awake the first three hours of the night one obtains the result of performing an agnistoma sacrifice. By remaining awake the first six hours of the night one obtains the result of performing a Vajpeya sacrifice. By remaining awake the first nine hours of the night one obtains the result of performing an Aśvamedha sacrifice and by remaining awake the entire night one obtains the result of a Rājasūya sacrifice. On the day of Dvādaśī, or the day after Ekādaśī one should complete his vow by feeding the Vaiṣṇavas and the *brāhmaṇas*. A person who observes this Ekādaśī in this way certainly attains liberation."

Lord Kṛṣṇa continued, "O sinless one! According to your inquiry I have thus explained the procedure for observing the Padminī Ekādaśī. Now please hear about an enchanting story which Pulastya Muni once narrated to Nārada Muni.

"Once Kārtavīryārjuna defeated Rāvaṇa and put him in the prison house. When Pulastya Muni saw Rāvaṇa in this condition he went to Kārtavīryārjuna and requested him to release Rāvaṇa. Being requested by the great sage, the King finally released Rāvaṇa. Upon hearing about this amazing event, Nārada Muni humbly asked Pulastya Muni, 'O best of the sages! Since Rāvaṇa defeated all the demigods including Indra how could Kārtavīryārjuna defeat Rāvaṇa! Please explain this to me.'

"Pulastya Muni replied, 'O Nārada! In Tretā-yuga there was a king named Kṛtavīrya who took birth in the dynasty of Haihaya. His capital was Māhiṣmatīpuri. King Kṛtavīrya had one thousand wives but he had no suitable son to take over the reign of the kingdom. Although the King worshiped the forefathers, saintly persons and observed various vows under the guidance of the saintly person, still he was not blessed with a son. So the King decided to undergo austerities. The King entrusted the responsibility of his kingdom to his prime minister and set out to the forest to undergo austerities while wearing a dress made of bark. When he was about to live his palace one of his wives Padminī, the daughter of King Hariścandra, who appeared in the royal family of King Ikṣvāku, saw him. When the chaste wife saw her husband going to the forest to perform austerities she immediately gave up all her ornaments. She then accompanied her husband to the Mandara Mountain.

"At the summit of Mandara Mountain, King Kṛtavīrya and his wife Padminī performed severe austerities for ten thousand years. Upon seeing that her husband's body was becoming thin day by day the chaste wife thought of a solution. Padminī humbly asked the greatly chaste Anusuya, the wife of sage Atri, 'O chaste lady! My husband has spent ten thousand years in performing austerities yet he could not please Lord Keśava who destroys one's miseries. O fortunate one! Please tell me about a vow I can follow so that the Supreme Lord will be pleased and I will be blessed with a son who will become a powerful king.' Being pleased by the prayer of chaste Queen Padminī, Anusuya said, 'After every thirty-two months an extra leap year month comes. The two Ekādaśīs of this month are known as Padminī and Parama. If you observe this Ekādaśī then very soon the Supreme Lord will be pleased with you and award your desired result.'"

Lord Kṛṣṇa continued, "According to the instruction of Anusuya, Queen Padminī duly observed this Ekādaśī. Then Lord Keśava riding on the back of Garuḍa, came before Padminī and ordered her to ask for a benediction. The queen first offered her obeisances to the Lord and offered prayers. Then she requested the Lord to bless them with a son. Then the Lord said, 'O gentle lady! I am very pleased with you. There is no month as dear to me as the month of Adhika Masa or leap year month. The Ekādaśīs of this month are most dear to me. You have properly observed this Ekādaśī. Therefore I will certainly fulfill the desire of your husband.'

"After speaking in this way to Padminī, the Lord came before the King and said, 'O great King, please ask for your desired benediction. I have been pleased by your wife for she observed the sacred vow of Ekādaśī.' On hearing this words of Viṣṇu, the King became jubilant and begged the Lord to give him a son who would be very powerful and always victorious. He said, 'O Madhusūdana, the Lord of the universe, let me have a son who will not be defeated by the demigods, human beings, serpents or demons. 'Then Lord granted the King his desired boon and disappeared.

"Being fully satisfied, the King and his wife regained their health and returned to their opulent kingdom. In due course of time the Queen Padminī gave birth to a powerful son who became famous as Kārtavīryārjuna. There was no other warrior in the three worlds as great as him. Even the ten-headed Rāvaṇa was defeated by him.' After narrating this wonderful story the great sage Pulastya left."

Lord Kṛṣṇa concluded, "O sinless King! I have thus described to you the glories of the Ekādaśī which occurs during the waxing moon of an extra leap year month. O best of kings! Anyone who will observe this Ekādaśī will certainly go to the abode of Lord Hari."

According to the statement of Śrī Kṛṣṇa, Mahārāja Yudhiṣṭhira with his entire family observed this Ekādaśī. A person who faithfully observes this Padminī Ekādaśī during his life becomes glorious. Even one who hears or reads the glories of this Ekādaśī obtains a great amount of piety.

Chapter 26

Parama Ekādaśī

The glories of Parama Ekādaśī, which occurs during the waning moon on an extra leap year month, are described by Lord Kṛṣṇa to Mahārāja Yudhiṣṭhira.

Mahārāja Yudhiṣṭhira said, "O my Lord! What is the name of the Ekādaśī which occurs during the waning moon on an extra leap year month and what is the procedure for observing this Ekādaśī?'

Lord Kṛṣṇa replied, "O King! The name of this Ekādaśī is Parama Ekādaśī. This auspicious Ekādaśī destroys all one's sinful reactions and awards one material enjoyment and liberation. The procedure for observing this Ekādaśī is the same as I have already described to you. One should worship the Supreme Lord who is the master of all beings on this Ekādaśī. Now please hear an enchanting story which I had heard from the sages in the city of Kampilya.

"There was a pious *brāhmaṇa* named Sumedha who lived in the city of Kampilya and who had a chaste wife named Pavitrā. But due to some sinful activities this *brāhmaṇa* became poor. He could not earn his livelihood even by begging. Eventually he had no food to eat, no cloth to wear, and no place to sleep. Nevertheless his young beautiful wife faithfully served him. Often she had to remain hungry for the sake of serving a guest. In spite of often remaining hungry her face did not become pale. She never told her husband about this.

"But upon seeing that his wife was becoming weaker day by day, the *brāhmaṇa* condemned himself and said to his sweet speaking wife, 'O dear one! Although I have tried to beg from the most influential people, I did not get anything. Now tell me what should I do? Should I go to a foreign country to earn wealth? I may get something there if I am fortunate. Without enthusiasm, no work is successful. That is why intelligent persons always praise the enthusiasm of the people.'

"After hearing these words of her husband, Sumedha, the beautiful eyed Pavitrā said to him with folded hands and tears in her eyes, 'There is no one more intelligent than you. Whatever we do and whatever we achieve in this world is due to our previous deeds. If one has no piety accumulated from his previous life, he cannot attain anything, however hard he may try. If a person distributes knowledge or wealth in his previous life, he attains similar things in this life. O best of the *brāhmaṇas*! It seems that neither you nor I gave any charity to a suitable candidate in our previous lives, and that is why both of us will have to stay here together. O Lord! I cannot remain without you even for a movement. Moreover, if you go, then people will call me an unfortunate person and will condemn me. Therefore please be happy with whatever wealth you can collect here. You will certainly achieve happiness in this country only.'

"Upon hearing these words of his wife, the *brāhmaṇa* dropped his plan to go to a foreign country. One day by Providence the great sage Kauṇḍinya Muni came there. As soon as Sumedha saw him, he and his wife became joyful and offered their obeisances to the sage. He offered an *āsana* to the sage and worshiped him properly. He said, 'O great sage! Today our lives have become successful for we have received your *darśana*. Then the couple fed the sage according to their ability. Then the wife of the *brāhmaṇa* asked, 'O learned sage! What is the means of destroying poverty? Without giving any charity how can one get wealth, education and so on? My husband wanted to go to a foreign country in order to earn wealth but I have stopped him from this act. It is indeed our good fortune that you have come here. By your mercy our poverty will certainly be destroyed. Now please instruct us so that our poverty will be destroyed.'

"After hearing these words from Pavitrā, the great sage Kauṇḍinya said, 'There is an auspicious Ekādaśī which occurs during the waning moon on the extra leap year month. This Ekādaśī is very dear to the Lord and it is known as Parama Ekādaśī. This Ekādaśī vanquishes one's sinful reactions, material miseries and poverty. By observing this Ekādaśī a person certainly become prosperous. This sacred Ekādaśī was first observed by Kuvera. As a result of this, Lord Śiva became pleased and awarded him the benediction of becoming very rich. By observing this Ekādaśī, King Hariścandra regained his kingdom and wife whom he once sold out. O beautiful eyed one! You should also observe this Ekādaśī.'

Lord Kṛṣṇa continued, "O Pāṇḍava! After happily and affectionately describing the topics of Parama Ekādaśī, Kauṇḍinya Muni described the auspicious vow known as Pañcarātri. By observing the Pañcarātri vow one attains liberation. One should begin to observe the Pañcarātri vow from the day of Parama Ekādaśī with proper rules and regulations. Anyone who according to his ability fasts for five days beginning from Parama Ekādaśī goes back to the abode of Lord Viṣṇu along with his father, mother and wife. One who eats only once a day during these five days becomes free from all sinful reactions and goes to the spiritual world.'

"According to the instructions of Kauṇḍinya Muni, both husband and wife duly observed this Parama Ekādaśī. When the vows of Ekādaśī and Pañcarātri were completed, a prince from the royal palace came there. Being inspired by Lord Brahmā the prince offered them a new house decorated with beautiful royal furniture. He also gave a cow to the *brāhmaṇa* for their livelihood and after praising the *brāhmaṇa* couple the prince left. As a result of this, this prince returned to the abode of Viṣṇu at the end of his life.

"As the *brāhmaṇas* are best among the human beings, as the cows are best among the four-legged animals, as Indra is the best among the demigods, similarly the leap year month is the best among all the months. Within this month the two Ekādaśīs namely Padminī and Parama are most dear to Lord Hari. If after receiving a human form of life one does not observe Ekādaśī, then he never attains any happiness throughout the eight million, four hundred thousand species of life. Rather he suffers unlimited miseries. By virtue of great piety one obtains a human birth, therefore one should certainly observe the vow of Ekādaśī."

After hearing the glories of this Ekādaśī, Mahārāja Yudhiṣṭhira along with his wife and brothers observed this sacred Ekādaśī.

Appendix

The glories of Ekādaśī described in *Garga-saṁhitā*

Nārada Muni said, "O Maithila! Please hear the topics about the *gopīs,* for such topics destroy all one's sinful activities, award piety, fulfill all one's desires, and are the source of all auspiciousness.

"In South India there is country named Ushinara, where there was no rainfall for ten years. The prosperous cowherd men of this place became afraid of the severe drought and they left for Vraja-mandala along with their relatives and cows. O King! They came and lived at the transcendental abode of Vṛndāvana near the Yamunā under the guidance of Nanda Mahārāja. By the benediction of Rāmacandra, many *gopīs* took birth in their families. They were all transcendentally beautiful and decorated with fresh youth. O best of kings! After seeing beautiful Kṛṣṇa, these gopis became enchanted, and in order to know how to please Kṛṣṇa, they approached Śrī Rādhā.

"The *gopīs* said, 'O Radhe! O daughter of King Vrisabhanu! O lotus-eyed one! Please instruct us about a vow by which we can please Śrī Kṛṣṇa. The son of Nanda Mahārāja, Kṛṣṇa, who is rarely attained even by the demigods, is under Your control. O Radhe! You are the enchanter of the entire universe and are expert in all the scriptures.'

"Śrī Rādhā said, 'You should observe Ekādaśī in order to please Śrī Kṛṣṇa. Then the Lord will certainly be controlled, there is no doubt about it.' The *gopīs* said, 'O Radhike! Please tell us the names of all the Ekādaśīs that occur during a full year and how one should observe Ekādaśī.' Rādhā replied, 'Ekādaśī first appeared from the body of Lord Viṣṇu during the waning moon in the month of November/December in order to kill the demon Mura. This exalted Ekādaśī appeared every month in different forms. For your benefit I am describing their names: Utpannā, Mokṣadā, Saphalā, Putradā, Ṣaṭ-tilā, Jayā, Vjayā, Āmalakī, Papamochani,

Kāmadā, Varuthinī, Mohinī, Aparā, Nirjalā, Yoginī, Devasayani, Kaminī, Pavitrā, Aja, Padma, Indirā, Pāśāṅkuśā, Ramā, and Prabodhini. These are the twenty-four Ekādaśīs that occur during one complete year. Apart from them, there are two more Ekādaśīs, namely Padminī and Parama, which occur during the extra month in a leap year. Anyone who chants the names of these twenty-six Ekādaśīs obtains the result of observing the vow of Dvādaśī for the entire year.

"'O *gopīs* of Vraja! Now hear about the rules and regulations for observing Ekādaśī. On the day before Ekādaśī one should sleep on the floor, eat only once, and control the senses. He should also drink water only once and remain neat and clean. On the day of Ekādaśī one should rise early in the morning during Brahma muhurta and offer obeisances to Lord Hari. To take bath with well water is the lowest, to take bath in a pond is medium, to take bath in a large pool is the highest, and to take bath in a river is the best of all. A pious person should take bath in this way and give up his anger and greed. One should not apply oil on the day of Ekādaśī. A person should give up associating with low-class sinners and atheists on the day of Ekādaśī. A person who is observing the vow should carefully avoid the association of those who speak lies, who blaspheme the *brāhmaṇas*, who steal others' things, who enjoy the association of others' wives, who are miscreants, and who do not show respect to exalted personalities. On the day of Ekādaśī one should worship Lord Keśava with devotion and offer Him palatable foodstuffs, one should offer lamps in the temple of the Lord. One should hear the glories of the vow from the mouth of a *brāhmaṇa* and then give him sufficient *dakṣīṇa*. One should remain awake on the night of Ekādaśī while singing the transcendental glories of Kṛṣṇa. One should avoid eating in a bell metal plate, eating meat, pink dal, any kind of intoxicant, spinach, honey, preboiled rice, eating more then once and indulging in sex life on the day before Ekādaśī. On the day of Ekādaśī one should give up gambling, sleeping, eating betelnuts and pan, brushing teeth, criticizing others, cheating, stealing, becoming envious, indulging in sex life, becoming angry and speaking lies. On the day of Dvādaśī one should not eat from a bell metal plate and one should not eat urad dal, honey, oil, and contaminated foodstuff. One should strictly follow these rules and regulations.'

"The *gopīs* said, 'O greatly learned one! Please explain to us the proper time for observing Ekādaśī.'

"Śrī Rādhā replied, 'If the *tithi* of Daśamī consists of fifty-five dandas then one should not fast on the next day, rather he should fast on the day of Dvādaśī. If an Ekādaśī is conjoined by a fraction of a second with Daśamī, then such an Ekādaśī should be rejected like a pot of Ganges water mixed with a drop of wine. If an Ekādaśī extends into the day of Dvādaśī, then one should fast on the day of Dvādaśī. O damsels of Vraja, by hearing the glories of Ekādaśī one obtains the result of performing a Vajpayee sacrifice. The result one obtains by following a vow of a Dvādaśī is equal to that of feeding 88,000 *brāhmaṇas*. By observing the vow of Ekādaśī one obtains one thousand times more results then the result one obtains by donating the entire earth with all the oceans and forests. Observing the vow of Dvādaśī is advised as the means of deliverance for those who are absorbed in the ocean of material existence which is filled with the mire of sinful activities. If human beings observe Ekādaśī by remaining awake on the night of Ekādaśī then even if they are very sinful they do not go to the fearful abode of Yamarāja.

"'A person who worships Lord Hari with devotion on the day of Dvādaśī by offering Him Tulasi leaves never becomes touched by sin just as a lotus leaf remains untouched by water. The result of performing one thousand horse sacrifices and one hundred Rājasūya sacrifices is not even equal to the one sixteenth portion of the result obtained by observing Ekādaśī. By observing Ekādaśī a person delivers ten generations of his mother's family, ten generation from his father's family and ten generations from his wife's family. A cow may be a white or black, but both are qualitatively the same because they both give milk. Similarly the Ekādaśīs of both the waning moon and waxing moon are the same in awarding piety.

"'O *gopīs*! An Ekādaśī burns to ashes heaps of sinful reactions that a person accumulates over one hundred lifetimes. The charity given on the day of Dvādaśī, though it may be less or more and given with or without proper rules and regulations, awards merits equal to that of a mountain. A person who hears the topics of Hari on the day of Ekādaśī obtains the result of giving the entire earth, which consists of seven islands, in charity. The piety one achieves by taking bath in the holy place of Gayā and seeing the lotus feet of Lord Viṣṇu is not even equal to the one sixteenth portion of piety obtained by observing Ekādaśī. The merit one obtains by giving charity at Prabhasa-kṣetra, Kurukṣetra, Kedarnātha, Badrikāśrama, Kashi, Sukaraksetra, during the solar and lunar eclipse, as well as giving charity during four hundred thousand Sankrantis (when the sun enters into a particular rasi) is not even equal to one sixteenth portion of merit one obtains by fasting on Ekādaśī.'

"Sri Rādhā continued, 'O *gopīs*! Just as Ananta is best among the snakes, Garuḍa is best among the birds, Lord Viṣṇu is best among the demigods, the *brāhmaṇa* is best among the varnas, the banyan tree is best among the trees, and Tulasi is best among the leaves, similarly the vow of Ekādaśī is best among all the vows. The result one obtains by performing austerities for ten thousand years is obtained simply by observing the vow of a Dvādaśī. O damsels of Vraja! Such are the glories of the vow of Ekādaśī. All of you should immediately observe this vow.'

"The *gopīs* said, 'O beautiful one! O daughter of King Vrisabhanu! You are expert in all scriptures. Even the statement of Brihaspati is baffled before Your statement. O Radhe! You are directly the ocean of transcendental knowledge. Please describe to us particularly the names of those who have previously observed these Ekādaśīs.'

"Rādhā replied, 'O *gopīs*! In order to regain their lost kingdom, the demigods observed this sacred Ekādaśī long, long ago. King Vaishanta observed this Ekādaśī in order to deliver his forefather from the abode of Yamarāja. The sinful King Lumpaka, who was rejected by his subjects, observed the vow of Ekādaśī and regained his lost kingdom. King Ketumana of Badravati, who had no son, observed the vow of Ekādaśī according to the instruction of the learned *brāhmaṇas* and was blessed with a son. Once the wives of the demigods instructed the wife of one *brāhmaṇa* to observe Ekādaśī. Though that wife of the *brāhmaṇa* was an ordinary human being, she achieved prosperity and heavenly pleasure. Both

Puṣpadanta and Malyavan became ghosts due to being cursed by their enemies, but by observing the vow of Ekādaśī they regained their original forms as Gandharvas. In ancient times in order to built a bridge on the ocean and to kill Rāvaṇa, Rāmacandra observed this Ekādaśī. At the end of the annihilation, the demigods observed the vow of Ekādaśī under an *āmalakī* tree for the benefit of the entire world.

"'Sage Medhavi observed the vow of Ekādaśī according to the instruction of his father and became freed from the bad association of the Apsarās and thus became fully effulgent. A Gandharva named Lalit became a demon by the curse of his wife, but by observing this Ekādaśī he regained his position as a Gandharva. By observing the vow of Ekādaśī many great kings like Mandata, Sagara, Kakutstha, Mucukunda, and Dhundhumara went back to the spiritual world. By observing Ekādaśī, Lord Śiva became freed from the curse of Brahmā. A son of a *vaiśya* named Dhṛṣṭabuddhi returned to Vaikuṇṭha by observing this Ekādaśī. King Rukmangada also observed the vow of Ekādaśī, and as a result he enjoyed the whole world as his kingdom and at the end of life he returned to Vaikuṇṭha with his subjects. King Ambarisa also observed this Ekādaśī and as a result even the inevitable curse of Lord Brahmā could not touch him. A Yakṣa named Hema Mali became afflicted by leprosy due to the curse of Kuvera, but by observing the vow of Ekādaśī he became as good as the moon. By observing Ekādaśī, King Mahījit was blessed with a son and at the end of his life returned to Vaikuṇṭha.

"'In Satya-yuga there was a king named Shobhana, who became the son-in-law of King Mucukunda. He observed Ekādaśī and attained a beautiful place among the demigods in Mandara Mountain. Even today he is ruling his kingdom, just like Kuvera, with his wife, Candrabhaga. O *gopīs*! Know for certain that the vow of Ekādaśī is the highest of all. There is no *tithi* as auspicious as the *tithi* of Ekādaśī.'"

Nārada Muni concluded, "After hearing this description from Śrī Rādhā the *gopīs* properly observed the Ekādaśī in order to attain the favor of Kṛṣṇa. As a result of their observing Ekādaśī Lord Hari became pleased with them and performed *rāsa* dance with them on the full moon night in the month of Agrahayana (November).

The necessity for observing the eight Mahā-dvādaśīs

In this regard one should also know the topics of the eight Mahā-dvādaśīs. These topics are described in the *Brahma-vaivarta Purāṇa* in the conversation between Śrī Sūta Gosvāmī and Śaunaka Ṛṣi.

Sri Sūta Gosvāmī said, "O learned *brāhmaṇa*! Unmīlinī, Vyañjulī, Trispṛśā, Pakṣavardhinī, Jayā, Vijayā, Jayanti, and Pāpanāśinī are the eight Mahā-dvādaśīs. They are most auspicious and destroy all one's sinful reactions. Among these eight Mahā-dvādaśīs, the first four occur according to the *tithi,* or day, and the later four occur according to *nakṣatra*, or star. Nevertheless all of them destroy heaps of sinful reactions.

The eight Mahā-dvādaśīs are described as follows:

1. If an Ekādaśī extends on the day of Dvādaśī, but the day of Dvādaśī does not extend then it is called Unmīlinī Mahā-dvādaśī. It destroys all one's sinful reactions.

2. If an Ekādaśī does not extend to the day of Dvādaśī, but the day of Dvādaśī extends into the day of Trayodaśī, then it is called Vyañjuli Mahā-dvādaśī. It counteracts unlimited sins.

3. If an Ekādaśī extends up to sunrise on the day of Dvādaśī and the Dvādaśī extends up to the sunrise of Trayodaśī, then it is called Trispṛśā Mahā-dvādaśī. This Mahā-dvādaśī is extremely dear to Lord Hari. (But if the above-mentioned Ekādaśī is conjoined with Daśamī then it will not be a Trispṛśā Mahā-dvādaśī).

4. If an Amāvasyā or Pūrṇimā extends then the Dvādaśī which comes prior to them is known as Pakṣavardhinī Mahā-dvādaśī. Instead of observing a fast on Ekādaśī one should observe fast on that Dvādaśī.

These above-mentioned four Dvādaśīs are ascertained according to the conjunction of the days.

5. It is stated in the *Brahma Purāṇa* in the conversation between sage Vasiṣṭha and King Mandata that if the *nakṣatra* called Punarvasu touches the day of Dvādaśī of the waxing moon then it is

called Jayā Mahā-dvādaśī. This Mahā-dvādaśī is most auspicious among all the *tithis*.

6. It is written in *Viṣṇu-dharmottara* that when Śravaṇa-nakṣatra conjoins with the Dvādaśī of the waxing moon it is called Vijayā Mahā-dvādaśī. Since Śrī Vāmanadeva appeared during Śravaṇa-nakṣatra this Mahā-dvādaśī is unlimitedly glorious. Moreover, if such a Mahā-dvādaśī occurs on a Wednesday in the month of August, then its glories are indescribable. On that day one should particularly discuss the topics of Śrī Vāmanadeva.

7. If a Dvādaśī of the waxing moon is conjoined with Rohini-nakṣatra, then it is the all-auspicious Jayanti Mahā-dvādaśī. It destroys all one's sinful reactions. Since Lord Kṛṣṇa appeared during Rohini-nakṣatra, this Jayanti Mahā-dvādaśī is extremely glorious. On this day one should discuss the pastimes of Lord Kṛṣṇa's birth, etc.

8. It is stated in the *Brahma Purāṇa* that if a Dvādaśī of the waxing moon is conjoined with Puṣya-nakṣatra, then it is called Pāpanāśinī Mahā-dvādaśī. By observing a fast on this day, one can obtain the result of observing one thousand Ekādaśīs. If this Pāpanāśinī Mahā-dvādaśī occurs in the month of March, then it awards unlimited piety.

Although various results of these vows are described in the scriptures, an intelligent pure devotee should totally give up the desire for results that aim at fulfilling their own sense gratification and aspire for pure devotional service, which aims at gratifying Kṛṣṇa's senses. He should consider love of God as the supreme goal of life.

Whenever these eight Mahā-dvādaśīs arrive, the pure devotees should protect the prestige of Mahā-dvādaśī, even if they have to give up the previous Ekādaśī. By observing a Mahā-dvādaśī, the observance of Ekādaśī is automatically completed and Lord Hari will also be greatly pleased.

The instructions of Śrī Mahāprabhu regarding Ekādaśī

One day after visiting the Gundica temple, Gaurahari came and sat down in the Jagannātha Vallabha garden. It was the day of a sacred Ekādaśī. The Lord spent the entire day and night chanting the holy names of Kṛṣṇa, accompanied by many resident devotees like Svarūpa Dāmodara, Rāmānanda Rāya, and Vakreśvara Paṇḍita.

The Lord said, "Today all of you should attentively chant the holy names of Kṛṣṇa and give up eating and sleeping. Some of you should chant the holy names a prescribed number of rounds, some of you should offer obeisances, and some of you should discuss the topics of Kṛṣṇa and Balarāma. Stay anywhere and constantly chant the name of Govinda and always be intoxicated with love of God."

At that time Gopinātha, along with Sarvabhauma Bhaṭṭācārya, brought *prasāda* from Gundica temple. They placed rice, various types of vegetables, sweets, sweet rice, yogurt, and curd before Mahāprabhu. By the order of the Lord everyone offered obeisances and repeatedly glorified the *mahā-prasāda*. Then they spent the entire day and night chanting the holy names of the Lord without any offence. According to the instruction of the Lord they took bath early in the morning on the day of Dvādaśī and broke the Ekādaśī fast with *mahā-prasāda*.

Thereafter the devotees folded their hands and requested the Lord as follows. "O Lord! We know that the vow of Ekādaśī is the crest jewel among all the vows. We strictly observe this vow by giving up eating and sleeping. But it is recommended that the grain *prasāda* of Jagannātha which is always respected at Jagannātha Purī should be honored immediately upon receiving it. Therefore O Lord! We are in a great dilemma and also frightened. Please instruct us clearly in this regard. We know that your orders are the statements of the *Vedas* and they are followed even by Lord Brahmā and Lord Śiva."

The Lord replied, "Observing Ekādaśī is one of the limbs of devotional service. If one does not follow Ekādaśī, his spiritual life will be spoiled. One should simply respect the *prasāda* on the day of Ekādaśī and eat them on the next day. On the day of Ekādaśī the pious Vaiṣṇavas should become satisfied by drinking the nectar of Kṛṣṇa's holy names. They do not indulge in any kind of material enjoyments and do not speak any useless words. The pure Vaiṣṇavas only honor foodstuffs that have already been offered to the Lord and do not eat any unoffered foodstuff. On the day of sacred Ekādaśī they fast totally and they break their fast by eating *prasāda* on the next day. Only in special circumstances do Vaiṣṇavas accept nongrain foodstuffs on the day of Ekādaśī. Those who are nondevotees enjoy various foodstuffs day and night on the pretext of eating *prasāda*. Such people associate with sinful persons and eat grains on the day of Ekādaśī. Always cultivate the limbs of devotional service and thereby respect Bhakti-devī and you will obtain her bhakti. Give up the association of nondevotees and observe the vow of Ekādaśī.

"Consider carefully that actually there is no contradiction between honoring *prasāda* and observing Ekādaśī. Know for certain that if a person accepts one limb and envies another limb, he is certainly a fool. One should strictly follow a particular limb of devotional service according to time, place, and circumstance. The son of Nanda Mahārāja is the Lord of all the limbs. Therefore please follow that by which He becomes pleased. One must give up eating and sleeping on the day of Ekādaśī and honor *prasāda* only on the next day."

After hearing these words of the Lord, all the Vaiṣṇavas happily chanted the name Govinda and offered their respectful obeisances to Him. All the devotees of Orissa and Bengal headed by Svarūpa Dāmodara and Rāmānanda Rāya became jubilant.

End of Ekādaśī Māhātmya